Utopia

Other books by the same author:

London Writing
Psychogeography
Occult London
The Art of Wandering
South

Utopia

MERLIN COVERLEY

POCKET ESSENTIALS

This edition published in 2016
First published in 2010 by Pocket Essentials
PO Box 394, Harpenden, Herts, AL5 1XJ
www.pocketessentials.com

ISBN
978-1-84243-316-4 (Print)
978-1-84243-873-2 (epub)

2 4 6 8 10 9 7 5 3

Typeset by Avocet Typeset, Somerton, Somerset TA11 6RT
Printed and bound in Great Britain by Clays Ltd, St Ives plc

To Orla

Contents

Introduction

By then I had realised — and if I had not, I would have been singularly obtuse — that the idea of a perfect world had, through the ages, embedded itself inextricably in the feelings of the human race. The more I searched for examples, definitions and hopes, the more all-enveloping did the idea become. The range of utopias was, as far as I could see, infinite, and any kind of catalogue would have been impossible, if only because utopias are, amoeba-like, capable of indefinitely dividing themselves in half. Bernard Levin, *A World Elsewhere*[1]

Utō'pǐa (ū) *n*. Imaginary place with perfect social and political system; ideally perfect place or state of things. [title of book by More (1516), mod. L, = nowhere, f. Gk *ou* not + *topos* place; see –IA][2]

Judged on the brief definition above, the concept of utopia at first appears reassuringly straightforward – a perfect but imaginary place – and one which we all recognise. And yet on closer inspection this term reveals itself to be something rather more ambiguous. *Utopia* is, of course, the name Sir Thomas More created for his book of 1516. But More's title combines two Greek neologisms, *outopia*, meaning no-place, and *eutopia*, meaning good-place, to create a word that is also a pun, and a place that is simultaneously good and non-existent. As a consequence, later writers have attempted to coin a term to suggest the opposite, a bad but equally imaginary place. Firstly, Jeremy Bentham, in 1818, introduced the term *cacotopia*, meaning bad or worst place. But this was to be superseded by the term *dystopia*, first used by Bentham's younger colleague John Stuart Mill in an address to Parliament in 1868. Since then, however, there has been a further attempt to reclassify the growing multiplicity of utopian worlds by separating those which are intentionally dystopian from those which sought to be utopian but whose aims were somehow perverted. This latter group of utopias gone bad have become known since the 1960s as *anti-utopias*. Furthermore, in recent decades, new variants upon the utopian theme have begun to emerge. Amongst these are: *ecotopia*, an ecological utopia and the title of Ernest Callenbach's utopian novel of 1975; *e-topia*, the translation of utopia to the virtual realm; and finally *heterotopia*, Michel Foucault's puzzling notion of a place outside or between the categories of the physical and the mental whose otherness challenges our everyday understanding of time and place.

In this account I will be employing the term utopia in its broadest sense, as an umbrella under which accounts of imaginary worlds, good, bad, and most frequently both, take shelter alongside more practical attempts to make such dreams a reality. My emphasis here will be upon utopia as primarily a literary tradition, the precursors to which precede the publication of More's *Utopia* by more than two thousand years. As a literary genre, however, accounts of utopia are not restricted to the novel, a relatively recent addition to the utopian tradition, and one which is supplemented by poetry and polemic, apocalyptic visions and eye-witness statement. Of course, not every account of an imaginary place can qualify as utopian, and the entries here all offer a detailed and sustained attempt to outline a fully-realised alternate world. Equally importantly, such entries must capture the hopes and fears of their authors and the societies that produced them. Consequently, as historical fashions change, so one generation's utopia may, and almost always does, become the following generation's nightmare. Hence, the utopias of Plato and More, Owen and Wells, may well contain within them elements that appear sensible or even attractive but one would be challenged to find a contemporary reader willing to join the communities they envisaged.

Writing in his introduction to More's *Utopia* in 1965, Paul Turner notes that the utopian genre has since produced 'well over a hundred specimens, the last in 1962'.[3] Yet only fourteen years after the date of Turner's last example, in 1976, Lyman Tower Sargent's monumental *British and American Utopian Literature, 1516–1985: An Annotated, Chronological Bibliography* was to include more than 3,000 entries.[4] This vast discrepancy simply highlights the fact that a precise definition of what constitutes a utopia remains as elusive as ever. In recent years there have been myriad academic 'solutions' to this particular problem, often involving an attempt to judge the 'credibility' of a particular utopian narrative through an analysis of the types of social organisation it employs.[5] It is beyond the scope of this book to discuss such developments here, other than to note that any author compiling an overview of the utopian genre will quickly find himself in agreement with Bernard Levin's remarks above. For the more one immerses oneself in the utopian tradition the more one is made aware of its sheer scale and complexity, as the search for new examples reveals endless new lines of inquiry. Needless to say, any attempt to accommodate all, or even a substantial part, of the utopian canon in this account, would render it little more than an exercise in bibliography.

Instead, I have chosen to select a representative sample from those texts which have captured most clearly the utopian hopes and fears of their day. This selection is restricted to the Western literary tradition, although many of these narratives site their utopias far beyond the borders of the Western world, often within the then uncharted spaces of the southern hemisphere. Of course, several entries simply demand inclusion – it would be hard to envisage an overview of the utopian genre that omitted Plato's *Republic*, More's *Utopia*, or the works of Robert Owen and HG Wells. Elsewhere, however, I have chosen to discuss utopias more frequently overlooked in standard accounts of the genre: works such as Henry Neville's *The Island of Pines*, Louis De Bougainville's *Voyage Round the World*, and a more recent example, Derek Raymond's *A State of Denmark*. Inevitably in a project of this scope one is faced with awkward choices, particularly as one approaches congested periods such as the late nineteenth century, in which the production of utopias was to increase exponentially. Indeed, it soon becomes clear that for each utopia listed within these pages, many others have been omitted: so while Swift's eighteenth-century satire, *Gulliver's Travels*, has been included, Samuel Butler's nineteenth-century equivalent, *Erewhon*, has not; Rousseau's account of the noble savage has been overlooked in favour of Montaigne's essay *On Cannibals*; Charlotte Perkins Gilman's pioneering feminist utopia, *Herland*, has had to make way for Katherine Burdekin's equally ground-breaking dystopia, *Swastika Night*; while, amidst a positive glut of totalitarian nightmares from the twentieth century, Zamyatin's *We* and Orwell's *Nineteen Eighty-Four* have eclipsed Ray Bradbury's *Fahrenheit 451* and Anthony Burgess's *A Clockwork Orange*.

As an afterword to this book, I have briefly summarised current arguments surrounding the idea that utopia is an exhausted, or even dying concept. Despite, or perhaps as a result of this debate, however, publications on the subject of utopia in books, journals and online continue to grow. I have compiled a short selection of such material for further reading, and several of these titles are worthy of particular attention. *The Faber Book of Utopias* (1999), edited by John Carey and *The Utopia Reader* (1999), edited by Gregory Claeys and Lyman Tower Sargent, are the most accessible and informative single-volume overviews of the utopian literary tradition; both have proven an invaluable source of information. While Lyman Tower Sargent's colossal bibliography, mentioned above, remains the most comprehensive reference work upon the subject, this position is challenged by Mary Ellen Snodgrass's similarly exhaustive *Encyclopaedia of Utopian Literature*. For those seeking to understand the lasting influence exerted upon utopian ideas by the islands of the South Pacific, Neil Rennie's *Far Fetched Facts: The Literature of Travel and the Idea of the South Seas* provides the definitive account. Finally, Bernard

Levin's *A World Elsewhere* is a politically alert, and often very witty, history of the genre, born of a lifetime's reflection on the subject.

Notes

1 Bernard Levin, *A World Elsewhere*, London: Jonathan Cape, 1994, p. xvi.
2 *Concise Oxford Dictionary*, Sixth Edition (1976), ed. by JB Sykes, Oxford: Oxford University Press, 1976, p. 1282.
3 Paul Turner, ed. *Utopia*, Thomas More (1516), London: Penguin, 1965, Introduction, p. 16.
4 Lyman Tower Sargent, *British and American Utopian Literature, 1516–1985: An Annotated, Chronological Bibliography*, Boston: GK Hall, 1979.
5 For an account of two such attempts at definition, see Susan Bruce, ed., *Three Early Modern Utopias*, Oxford: Oxford University Press, 1999, Introduction, p. xii.

The Birth of Utopia: The Golden Age

The first eutopias we know of are myths that look to the past of the human race or beyond death for a time when human life was or will be easier and more gratifying. They have various labels — golden ages, Arcadias, earthly paradises, fortunate isles, isles of the blest. They are peopled with our earliest ancestors; heroes and, very rarely, heroines; the virtuous dead; or in some cases, contemporaneous but little-known noble savages...These utopias of sensual gratification are social dreaming at its simplest. Every culture has some such stories. Gregory Claeys & Lyman Tower Sargent.[1]

The term *Utopia* was coined by Thomas More in his work of 1516 and has spawned a vast literary tradition that continues to this day. And yet the desires and the fears which this term has come to encapsulate are to be found within the earliest forms of human expression, present in both the oldest examples of the written word, and no doubt originating in the oral traditions which preceded them. In the Western world, this utopian tradition anticipates More's celebrated text by more than 2,000 years, and it is rooted in the earliest myths of a golden age. Many of these myths are also to be found in the utopias of the Middle Ages, brought together through the intervening centuries by the crucial role of Christianity in shaping these early utopian longings into a coherent system of belief. The Christian millennium provides a utopian future towards which the believer may strive, while heaven awaits for the chosen few after death. But, in the pre-Christian era, utopias tended to describe a time long since passed, a lost age of earthly abundance to be contrasted with the hardships of the present. It is here that utopia was born, within tales of lost civilisations whose history continues to resonate today.

The Myth of Atlantis

The source of the Atlantis myth is commonly ascribed to Plato.[2] As the story goes, Egyptian priests told Solon, the semi-mythical Athenian poet and lawgiver who lived some three generations before Plato, about a city which had been destroyed by a cataclysmic flood some 9,000 years earlier – in around 9600BC.[3] First in the *Timaeus*, and later in the *Critias*, in which the island is described in some detail, Plato relates how Atlantis was founded by the god Poseidon, who fathered the island's first inhabitants in conjunction with the beautiful Cleito. This Atlantean civilisation was based upon a main island which also ruled over several lesser kingdoms on smaller islands and was, initially, at least, an earthly paradise of abundance and harmony. The historian of the occult, Jonathan Black, has provided the following summary of the Platonic account:

> The largest island was dominated by a beautiful and fertile plain and a large hill. Here Cleito lived, and the people enjoyed food which grew abundantly on the island. Two streams of water came up through the earth, one of hot water and one of cold.

To keep Cleito for himself, Poseidon had a series of circular canals dug around the hill. In time a sophisticated civilisation grew up, taming wild animals, mining metals and building – temples, palaces, racecourses, gymnasiums, public baths, government buildings, harbours and bridges. Many walls were coated with metals – with brass, tin and a red metal, unknown to us, called orichalcum. The temples had roofs of ivory and pinnacles of silver and gold. The islands of Atlantis were ruled over by ten kings each with his own kingdom, the nine others being subservient to the ruler of the largest island. The central temple, dedicated to Poseidon, had statues of gold, including one of the god standing in a chariot pulled by six-winged horses and flanked by hundreds of Nereids riding dolphins. Live bulls roamed freely around the forest of columns in this temple, and every five or six years the kings who ruled the islands were left alone in the temple to hunt these bulls without weapons. They would capture one, lead it up to the great column of orichalcum, inscribed with the laws of Atlantis, and there behead it.

Life on the islands of Atlantis was generally idyllic. In fact life was so good that eventually people could not bear it any longer and began to become restless, decadent and corrupt, searching after novelty and power. So Zeus decided to punish them. The islands were flooded until only small islets remained, like a skeleton sticking out of the sea. Then finally a great earthquake engulfed all that was left in the course of one day and one night.[4]

For Plato, the history of Atlantis is a cautionary tale, in which a society that could once boast perfection is gradually weakened by luxury and corruption, a process of degeneration through which this first utopia is gradually transformed into its opposite, a dystopia. Indeed, Plato contrasts the negative example of Atlantis with the ideal attributes of Athens, the society which was to attain greatness through its heroic struggle with Atlantis. In this light, Plato's Atlantis can be viewed as little more than a fairy tale, a device with which to bolster the foundation myth of Athens, and it has since been dismissed as a product of Plato's imagination. Aristotle implies precisely this when he claims, 'Plato alone made Atlantis rise out of the sea, and then he submerged it again.'[5] But Plato's account is corroborated by numerous other references to Atlantis throughout classical literature, from Proclus to Pliny, and Plutarch to Posidonius. Indeed, Plato's description finds further confirmation in other ancient cultures: 'The Aztecs recorded that they came from "Aztlan… the land in the middle of the water". Sometimes this land was called "Aztlan of the Seven Caves". It was depicted as a central, large step pyramid surrounded by six smaller pyramids. According to traditions collected by the invading Spaniards, humanity had nearly been wiped out by a vast flood…'[6] Certainly, Plato's date of 9600BC corresponds with that of the Aztecs, in placing this flood at around the end of the Ice Age. This lends the Atlantis legend both the support of modern geological science, as well as placing it within the wider context of biblical accounts of the Flood, which have been recounted across numerous other cultures.

The legend of Atlantis is a powerfully symbolic one, for there is no clear agreement as to its true location. Today, its existence acts as a shorthand for all those civilisations that time has erased but whose identity lives on in a kind of half-life, somewhere between the reassuring permanence of historical fact and the ethereal otherworldliness of myth. Furthermore, the destruction of Atlantis was an act of punishment, and here its utopian perfection can be identified as the very cause of its downfall, acting both as a rebuke against hubris and a reminder of the inherent dangers of the quest for human perfectibility: 'The Atlantis belief helps to perpetuate the idea of a multiplicity of worlds, all striving to attain perfection, seeking absolution for the sin that drowned their world and gradually growing nearer forgiveness through the ages.'[7]

The Golden Age

In the Epic of Gilgamesh, dating from the third millennium BC, Utnapishtim, Noah's Sumerian counterpart, describes a place called Dilmun, where 'the croak of the raven was not heard, the bird of death did not utter the cry of death, the lion did not devour, the wolf did not tear the lamb, the dove did not mourn, there was no widow, no sickness, no old age, no lamentation.'[8]

Of course, the literary myth of a primeval world of limitless abundance is a universal one, its Christian equivalent to be found in the Book of Genesis as the Garden of Eden. An anthropological explanation for the ubiquity of such imagery, in which fantasies about food predominate, appears to be that, contrary to common belief, early hunter-gatherer societies enjoyed both better nutrition and greater leisure than the primitive agriculturists which were to succeed them.[9] Because men and women were forced to abandon a way of life that was, relatively speaking, one of ease and plenty, in order to accommodate a higher density of population, these ancient dreams of the good life invariably display a retrogressive longing for a time now passed, a Golden Age never to be revisited.

This outlook was to find its most fervent expression in the poem *Works and Days*, by the Greek poet of the eighth century BC, Hesiod. A farmer's son living on the slopes of Mount Helicon in central Greece, and disenchanted with the unrelenting toil of his own age, Hesiod imagines a long-lost era of prosperity in which men lived as gods, contrasting this Golden Age with the paucity of his own existence. In this way, Hesiod describes a process of gradual deterioration, as the Golden Age was to give way to a Silver Age and later a Bronze, as man's innate foolishness and warlike nature destroy the idyllic existence that he once enjoyed. Following the brief respite afforded by the Age of Heroes, Hesiod describes man's fall into the fifth and final age, his own Age of Iron, a time characterised by strife and hunger:

> Fifth is the race that I call my own and abhor.
> O to die, or be later born, or born before!
> This is the Race of Iron. Dark is their plight.
> Toil and sorrow is theirs, and by night
> The anguish of death and the gods afflict them and kill,

Though there's yet a trifle of good amid manifold ill.

An unhappy age made all the more difficult to bear through comparison with its golden forbear:

> The gods who own Olympus as dwelling-place
> deathless, made first of mortals a Golden Race
> (this was the time when Kronos in heaven dwelt)
> and they lived like gods and no sorrow of heart
>   they felt.
> Nothing for toil or pitiful age they cared,
> but in strength of hand and foot still unimpaired
> they feasted gaily, undarkened by sufferings
> They died as if falling asleep; and all good things
> were theirs, for the fruitful earth unstintingly bore
> unforced her plenty, and they, amid their store
> enjoyed their landed ease which nothing stirred
> loved by the gods and rich in many of herd.[10]

Bernard Levin has argued that it is better to read Hesiod's poem backwards, his tragic lament for that which has been lost (but which, of course, had never been) characteristic of a pessimistic strand of utopianism which chooses to romanticise the past at the expense of the present.[11] The baleful consequence of yearning for something long gone (or never to arrive), is an entropic sense of time passed, a retrospective faith in past glories that can both emasculate the present and undermine the future. And yet this frustrated longing cannot so easily be discharged, and some six hundred years later, the Roman poet, Ovid, was to echo Hesiod's melancholic lament in his *Metamorphoses*:

In the beginning was the Golden Age, when men of their own accord, without threat of punishment, without laws, maintained good faith and did what was right. There were no penalties to be afraid of... indeed, there were no judges, men lived securely without them. Never yet had any pine tree, cut down from its home on the mountains been launched on ocean's waves, to visit foreign lands: men knew only their own shores...The peoples of the world, untroubled by any fears, enjoyed a leisurely and peaceful existence, and had no use for soldiers. The earth itself, without compulsion, untouched by the hoe, unfurrowed by any share, produced things spontaneously, and men were content with foods that grew without cultivation... It was a season of everlasting spring, when peaceful zephyrs, with their warm breath, caressed the flowers that sprang up without having been planted...Then there flowed rivers of milk and rivers of nectar, and golden honey dripped from the green holm-oak.[12]

Yet, if life remains hard and one can find solace only in the recall of a golden past, one may also look forward to an afterlife which, for some at least, will be spent in paradise. This paradise has, of course, been imagined in myriad forms and, in classical mythology, those favoured by the gods enjoyed their afterlife in the Elysian Fields or the Islands of the Blessed. The former, also known as the Elysian Plains or the Fields of Asphodel, were the final resting place of the heroic and the virtuous. The Elysian Fields lay on the Western boundary of the Earth and were encircled by the stream of Oceanus which, according to Homer in the *Odyssey* (8th century BC), 'sends up breezes of the West Wind blowing briskly for the refreshment of mortals.'[13] Hesiod refers to the Isles of the Blessed as lying in the Western Ocean, where the fortunate dead live a heavenly existence under the rule of Kronos, while the poet Pindar describes a single island whose inhabitants spend eternity, 'with horses and with wrestling; others with draughts; and with lyres; while beside them bloometh the fair flower of perfect bliss.'[14]

Indeed, islands, as John Carey has noted, tend to be the favoured form of paradises and utopias, perhaps because of the seclusion and sense of purity they provide. But such islands also recall the existence of the unborn human, marooned within the foetus, and so it has been claimed that the island may represent the deepest longings of the human for the protective fluid which once surrounded him.[15]

Lycurgus and the Spartans

If the Athens of Plato and Aristotle is remembered for its unparalleled cultural legacy, the adjective 'Spartan' today conveys the same virtues of endurance, frugality and simplicity by which this essentially military society was once defined. The father of the Spartan state, at least in the form which was to ensure its lasting fame, was the lawgiver Lycurgus, a semi-mythical figure about whom we know very little but whose exploits were later to be recorded by the Greek historian Plutarch (c. 46 -120 AD). In his *Life of Lycurgus*, Plutarch tells us that Sparta was refashioned under his leadership, a society of inequality and corruption transformed into one of shared ownership and rigorous militarism. And, as we shall see, if Plato's *Republic* appears to offer little comfort to its inhabitants and conforms to many people's idea of an authoritarian nightmare, the Sparta of Lycurgus proves an even more unlikely utopia, in which elements of free-love and communal living for the majority are offset by the existence of a brutally subjugated underclass.

Having seized power in a military coup, Lycurgus established a Senate of twenty-eight members and set about reversing the inequality which he identified as the source of 'insolence, envy, avarice and luxury.'[16] To this end, land-boundaries were cancelled and Sparta was redistributed amongst its citizens in 9,000 equal lots. Furthermore, gold and silver coinage was abolished and replaced by a currency measured in lengths of iron bars, which ended both corruption and the possibility of foreign trade. Sparta further enforced her own isolation by discouraging its citizens from travelling abroad (unless, it would seem, as part of an invading army). Allied to these radical economic sanctions was a collectivist drive that saw all Spartan men eat and live communally. Spartan women were also brought up to favour the state over the family, marrying on the basis of mutual consent while enjoying an unparalleled sexual freedom. And yet, in all societies that proclaim their egalitarian principles, some remain more equal than others, and Sparta was no exception. The Spartans were, 'in effect a leisured military caste. When they were not actually fighting, they spent their time dancing, hunting, training the young, or meeting to exercise or converse.

Work of any productive kind was forbidden to them.'[17] And, in an early example of a problem that has bedevilled many future utopias, the question arose as to who exactly was to undertake those menial tasks which nobody in an ideal society could envisage themselves doing. The solution here, as elsewhere, was to draft in a class of slaves who enjoyed none of the rights of citizens. In Lycurgus's Sparta, this underclass of slaves were known as the Helots and their role extended beyond merely cooking and cleaning to providing target practice for the training of young Spartan men, who were free to murder them with impunity.

In order to ensure the health of Sparta's future armies, all fathers were obliged to pass their newborn children to the elders who would examine them for signs of weakness. The sickly would be thrown into a deep cavern called the Apothetae, while those passed fit would, from the age of seven, begin a harsh regime of military training. The result of this policy of selective breeding and intensive training was that Sparta was swiftly propelled to a position of power that rivalled Athens, and today their military prowess is best remembered through the fabled exploits of the 300 Spartan soldiers who resisted the entire Persian army at Thermopylae. Momentarily, and for those of a certain temperament, it can be possible to romanticise this seemingly egalitarian world of martial virtue and domestic simplicity. Such thoughts are quickly dispelled, however, by returning to the details of Plutarch's account where the best antidote, perhaps, to nascent Sparta-worship, is the following description of the Spartan Wedding Night:

In their marriages, the bridegroom carried off the bride by violence – and brides were never of a tender age, but fully mature. When the time came, the woman who had direction of the wedding cut the bride's hair close to her scalp, dressed her in man's clothes, laid her upon a mattress and left her in the dark. The bridegroom – neither overcome with wine nor softened by luxury, but hardy and sober from always eating at the common table – went in privately, untied her girdle, and carried her to another bed. Having stayed there a short time, he modestly retired to his usual compartment, to sleep with the other young men. That is how the marriage would continue. The husband would spend the day with his men friends, and lie down with them at night, not even visiting his bride except with great caution, and apprehension at being discovered by the rest of her family.[18]

Plato, The Republic

Plato's proposals for the ideal society were not put into effect at Athens; but they festered through the centuries – some twenty-three centuries – to turn up again and again in a thousand forms. Those forms were – are – in essence one: they lay out the boundaries of freedom and forbid the citizens to cross the lines. Incessantly and repetitively, when rulers who are, or aspire, to being, absolute, their first action is to draw up laws, codes, obediences, salutes, threats – all to be followed scrupulously on pain of frightful punishments. Bernard Levin[19]

From a twenty-first century perspective, Plato's *Republic* (c. 360BC) is regarded both as the first systematic attempt to outline the ideal society and also as a blueprint for totalitarian government. For just as utopias reflect the historical epoch that gave rise to them, so too does their critical reception fluctuate over time. It is no surprise, therefore, to find that the one book which, more than any other, is responsible for identifying the authoritarian roots of Plato's utopia, Sir Karl Popper's *The Open Society and its Enemies* (Vol 1: The Spell of Plato), was first published in 1945. As the Second World War came to an end and the true nature of Nazi atrocities became apparent, the world sought to find the historical antecedents to totalitarian regimes both fascist and communist. Popper's work was extraordinarily influential in challenging the revered status of Plato's text, delivering a seemingly unanswerable attack from which the *Republic* has never fully recovered. And yet Utopian thinkers from Augustine to More, and HG Wells to Aldous Huxley, have all found much to admire in Plato's work, identifying with his emphasis upon a structured society and the rule of law as necessary bulwarks against the chaos and anarchy of social collapse.

Plato was born in around 427 BC into an aristocratic Athenian family and his *Republic* was born of his disillusionment with the failings of his own state, Athens. The humiliating defeat to Sparta in the Peloponnesian War was compounded in Plato's eyes by the restoration of democracy. For it was under democratic rule that Athens voted in 399 BC to put Socrates to death, on a trumped-up charge of impiety and corrupting the young. At this time Plato would have been a youth himself, and the death of his mentor marked a turning point in his life, as he rejected a political career in favour of the pursuit of 'true' philosophy:

> Finally I came to the conclusion that all existing states were badly governed, and that their constitutions were incapable of reform without drastic treatment and a great deal of good luck. I was forced, in fact, to the belief that the only hope of finding justice for society or for the individual lay in true philosophy, and that mankind will have no respite from trouble until either real philosophers gain political power or politicians become by some miracle true philosophers.[20]

This passage goes some way towards summarising the content of the *Republic*, whose title is somewhat misleading for a text that is concerned less with describing an ideal society than with the ideal man, the Philosopher Ruler, who will govern Plato's utopia. Consequently, much of the text is concerned with questions of ethics and education which, if successfully mastered, will allow Plato's ruling elite to govern wisely. In modern parlance, Plato's society will be governed as a 'Managerial Meritocracy', in which talent is recognised and put to its proper use.[21] The notion of a highly-trained ruling class, whose talents are put at the disposal of the society they govern, has proved an appealing one. The history of utopia is littered with examples of societies ruled by benevolent and selfless rulers whose wisdom allows them to make decisions on behalf of their less enlightened citizens. And yet such a faith in a ruling few often reveals a naive belief in the perfectibility of human nature, in which the corrupting influence of power is overlooked. In Plato's schema, the Philosopher Ruler discharges his responsibilities as a duty to society, and his philosophical training allows him a vision of reality denied to the uninitiated. However, the life envisaged by Plato for the Philosopher Ruler is by no means a universally attractive one. Strongly influenced by their rigid code of discipline and austerity, Plato's *Republic* demonstrates his admiration for the Spartans who had so comprehensively defeated his own Athenian people. As a result, both the Philosopher Rulers and the auxiliary class beneath them were required to turn their backs upon both private property and family life in favour of communal living in which wives and children are held in common and all forms of luxury are scorned. Those lucky enough to be chosen as future Rulers could look forward to a gruelling education comprising ten years of advanced maths followed by a further five years of philosophical training.[22]

The structure of Plato's society is rigidly ordered around a tripartite class division. Beneath the Rulers and Auxiliaries (collectively known as Guardians) lie the workers, and these strict divisions are reinforced by Plato's 'Noble Lie' through which the Rulers maintain the pretence that the classes are in fact physically different, the Gods having mixed gold in the composition of the Rulers, silver in the Auxiliaries, and iron and brass in the workers.[23] As usual, at the bottom of the pile lie the slaves. Plato doesn't specify what the gods mixed them with, placing them outside his class structure altogether, but one can guess what the common view was. At this time, slaves formed a third of the Athenian population, holding no civil rights, although in the *Republic* this role is reserved strictly for foreigners.[24]

At every level of Plato's *Republic* the dominant feature of human life is control from above: strict censorship is enforced to protect mental health; physical weakness and deformity are not tolerated; breeding is strictly controlled; family bonds are eradicated; private property is abolished; luxury is discouraged. Indeed, so revolutionary was Plato's conception of social life, it is almost impossible to imagine how such a society could ever become a reality. Plato certainly never gave up hope of training a statesman to become a Philosopher Ruler, but despite several attempts he remained unsuccessful.[25] It is not hard to see why, for as Plato's pupil, Aristotle, was to make clear, the major flaw in Plato's blueprint for the ideal society is his inability to account for the vagaries of human nature. Ultimately, Plato was unable to distinguish between loyalty for the state on the one hand, and family and individual relationships on the other, arguing that, in order to promote the former, one must diminish the latter. He was unable to realise that, rather than creating conflict, human relationships could also complement a wider allegiance to one's society. In short, as Aristotle maintained, he confused unity with uniformity.[26]

The most famous of Plato's works, the *Republic*, is less fully utopian in scope and detail than his final work, the *Laws*. Written in around 348 BC, the *Laws* provide a revised version of the *Republic*, retaining much of the broader philosophical framework of the earlier work but also revealing a much greater practical awareness and a detailed legislative programme. It is here that Plato offers a final confirmation of his unwavering belief in the rule of law, a principle which remains, some 2,000 years later, at the heart of political constitutions worldwide:

> I can see clearly that the state in which law is subject and without authority is on the brink of destruction. I see clearly that a state in which law is master of those in office, and those in office are slaves of law, enjoys security and all the other blessings which states receive from the gods.[27]

Saint Augustine, *City of God*

Plato's *Republic* remains the Western World's first and most revered example of a fully realised utopian (or dystopian) society. But its scale and ambition are more than matched by Saint Augustine's monumental *De Civitate Dei*, or *City of God* (c. 413–426 AD), written some seven centuries later. Unlike Plato's model for a perfect society here on Earth, Augustine's conception of the ideal is more concerned with the hereafter, where the individual will gain salvation after death through unity with God.

Aurelius Augustus (354–430 AD), or Saint Augustine as he was to become, was the foremost theologian of the early Christian Church, and his *City of God* is perhaps the greatest example of utopian millennialism, in which the ideal society is to be attained at the end of history. This point is to be reached at the conclusion of the struggle between good and evil, or the City of God and the City of Man: 'There are two cities, one of the wicked, the other of the holy, and both extend from the beginning of mankind to the end of time. Physically they intermingle; spiritually they are separate – and will further be physically separated on the day of judgement.'[28] The triumph of good will usher in a Christian commonwealth, an eternity of heavenly bliss: 'In the New Jerusalem, the redeemed will share with angels and ranks of saints a "house of the New Testament", a lustrous, glorious edifice studded with precious jewels, a permanent haven that will never fall to ruin.'[29]

Augustine's theological utopia runs to some twenty volumes and displays a determinist belief in the power of faith to uphold a Christian interpretation of past, present and future. And yet, while *City of God* attempts to describe, in painstaking detail, the precise nature of that godly municipality that lies in wait for the saved, it is also, like all utopias before and since, firmly grounded in the historical background of Augustine's own life and experiences.

Augustine was 56 when, in 410 AD, Rome was sacked by Alaric the Goth. And it is out of this event, and the end of the Roman Empire that it presaged, that *City of God* was written. Constructed over the remaining years of Augustine's life, *City of God* is a response to a new world order, in which the chaos and disorder of the pagan hordes are contrasted with the truth and love to be found in a society founded on Christian principles. The demise of Rome left a political and spiritual vacuum, and it is this that Augustine attempts to fill in *City of God*, providing future lawmakers and statesmen with a guide to avoiding the series of pitfalls that had conspired to destroy Rome.[30]

Yet while Augustine's society is plainly not divorced from life on Earth, it displays none of the faith in human institutions to be found in Plato's work. Instead, *City of God* attempts to translate a political outline of the state into a spiritual vision, in which the community is bound together not by shared allegiance to the state and its laws but by the common love and worship of God. As a consequence, each individual's own relationship to God outweighs any other allegiance, and the *City of God* reverses Plato's belief in the primacy of the state. This is not so much an ideal society as a community bound together by a personal commitment to, and faith in, an ideal – God. Ultimately, the *City of God* is populated by a community of believers whose allegiance to a higher principle renders them largely oblivious, if not acquiescent to, human affairs in which they appear to play little part. Here we have a utopia, which exists in tandem with the visible world of everyday existence, but which remains invisible to those without the faith that might grant them access. Augustine portrays the world as superficially indivisible but, in reality, the site of conflict between two warring cities, Jerusalem and Babylon, the City of Cain and that of Abel, the City of Man which contains all evil, and its heavenly counterpart, which is predestined to prevail and to reign eternally:

So this Heavenly City lives on earth as an alien; it secures its citizens from every nation; it gathers its alien community from every language; it cares nothing about differences of custom, legislation or organization, which contribute to the search for earthly peace and its maintenance; it does not abrogate or destroy any of these, but rather preserves and follows them... provided only that they do not stand in the way of the religious worship of the one true God.[31]

Despite Augustine's repeated emphasis upon the conflict between good and evil, City of God displays a curious passivity towards the human sphere, and a deeply conservative acceptance of the status quo. No doubt born of the turmoil he witnessed during his own lifetime as the old order was swept away, Augustine's City of God appears to call for an acceptance of human institutions, however flawed, in the understanding that compensation for worldly disappointment may be found in the hereafter. In addition, City of God demonstrates a problem that will, by definition, face any society that claims to have attained perfection, that of change. For as Lewis Mumford notes, 'The utopia of Christianity is fixed and settled: one can enter into the Kingdom of Heaven if a passport has been granted, but one can do nothing to create or mould this heaven. Change and struggle and ambition and amelioration belong to the wicked world, and bring no final satisfaction.'[32]

Mumford also remarks upon the fact that between Plato's Republic and Sir Thomas More's Utopia of 1516, a period of almost two thousand years, the idea of utopia appears to have fallen by the wayside. He describes Plutarch's Lycurgus and Augustine's City of God as largely unremarkable exceptions to this barren period, observing that 'while utopia dropt out of literature, it did not drop out of men's minds; and the utopia of the first fifteen hundred years after Christ is transplanted to the sky, and called the Kingdom of Heaven.'[33] In this respect, Augustine's City of God is symbolic of this 1,500-year lacuna in the fortunes of utopia, and it was not until the period of rapid change that characterised the late Middle Ages that such visions of a heavenly utopia were to be discarded in favour of more worldly concerns.

Notes

1 Gregory Claeys & Lyman Tower Sargent, eds., *The Utopia Reader*, New York: New York University Press, 1999, p.2.

2 For a scholarly account of the Atlantis legend as it appears in Plato's work, see Desmond Lee's 'Appendix on Atlantis' in his translation of Plato's *Timaeus and Critias*, Harmondsworth: Penguin, 1971, pp. 146–167.

3 Jonathan Black, *The Secret History of the World*, London: Quercus, 2007, p.161.

4 Black, *Secret History*, pp. 161–2.

5 Black, *Secret History*, p. 162.

6 Black, *Secret History*, p. 164.

7 Bernard Levin, *A World Elsewhere*, London: Jonathan Cape, 1994, p. 8.

8 *The Epic of Gilgamesh*, trans. by NK Sanders, Harmondsworth: Penguin, 1960, p. 39.

9 Pamela Neville-Sington and David Sington, *Paradise Dreamed: How Utopian Thinkers Have Changed the Modern World*, London: Bloomsbury, 1993, p. 4.

10 Hesiod, 'Works and Days', trans. by Jack Lindsay, in *The Oxford Book of Greek Verse in Translation*, ed. by TF Higham and CM Bowra, Oxford: Clarendon Press, 1938 and qtd. in Claeys and Sargent, p. 7.

11 Levin, p. 2.

[12] Ovid, *Metamorphoses* (I: 89–112), trans. by Mary M. Innes, Harmondsworth: Penguin, 1955, pp. 33–34.

[13] Homer, *The Odyssey*, trans. by Richard Lattimore, New York: Harper and Row, 1967 and qtd. in John Carey, ed., *The Faber Book of Utopias*, London: Faber, 1999, p. 11.

[14] *The Odes of Pindar Including the Principal Fragments*, trans. by Sir John Sandys, Cambridge MA: Harvard University Press, 1937, p. 591 and qtd. in Claeys and Sargent, p. 12.

[15] Carey, *Faber Book of Utopias*, p. 11.

[16] Carey, p. 24.

[17] Carey, p. 29.

[18] Plutarch, *Life of Lycurgus*, in *Ideal Commonwealths*, ed. by Henry Morley, London: Routledge, 1885, and qtd. in Carey, p. 29.

[19] Levin, p. 99.

[20] Plato, from the *Seventh Letter*, qtd. in Desmond Lee, 'Translator's Introduction', in *The Republic*, Harmondsworth: Penguin, 1974, p. 16.

[21] Desmond Lee, p. 50.

[22] Carey, p.13.

[23] Carey, p.12.

[24] Carey, p.12.

[25] For a brief account of these attempts, see Lee, p. 19–21.

[26] Aristotle, *Politics*, qtd. in Lee, p. 48.

[27] John Ferguson, *Utopias of the Classical World*, London: Thames & Hudson, 1975, p. 79.

[28] Ferguson, p. 184.

[29] Mary Ellen Snodgrass, *The Encyclopedia of Utopian Literature*, Santa Barbara, CA: Abc-Clio, 1995, p. 125.

[30] Snodgrass, p. 41.

[31] Ferguson, p. 187.

[32] Lewis Mumford, *The Story of Utopias: Ideal Commonwealths and Social Myths*, London: Harrap, 1923, p. 59.

[33] Mumford, p. 59

More, *Utopia*, and the Early Modern Era

The literary utopia had fallen into abeyance since Augustine's era some thousand years earlier, but the publication of Sir Thomas More's enduring classic revived the fortunes of the genre, becoming 'the fount for the outpouring of what we now call utopias.'[1] But, while these products of sixteenth-century England shared many of the themes that had characterised their classical forbears, *Utopia* and its many imitators were also markedly different in both form and content. Avoiding the temporal relocation of the Golden Age utopias in which ideal societies were products of a long since vanished epoch, or those millennial visions of a longed-for future, the utopian revival of the early modern era sought to establish these fictional locations firmly within the here and now. Furthermore, these utopias could no longer be dismissed as mere daydreams, for now their authors sought to offset fantasy with reality, inserting historical and autobiographical facts within the text and providing supporting apparatus such as maps, letters and, in More's case, even an alphabet, in attempts to sustain the credibility of their creations. Utopias had always been a reflection of the societies that had produced them but the border between fact and fiction was now less clear than ever before, as utopia became, for the first time, a plausible and fully realised destination.

Thomas More, *Utopia*

First published in Latin in Louvain in 1516, Thomas More's *Libellus vere aureus nec minus salutaris quam festivius de optimo reip[ublieae] statu, deq [ue] nova Insula Vtopia* was soon abbreviated to the more manageable *Utopia* by which it, and the genre it inaugurated, is known today. More than any other example of utopian literature, before or since, More's text has been subjected to the minutest critical scrutiny, as generations of readers have sought to unlock the text in search of the definitive interpretation. And yet *Utopia* has resolutely resisted such attempts, continuing to offer support for a seemingly contradictory range of beliefs and ideologies while refusing to reveal its author's true intentions. As a result, *Utopia* has been identified as both a symbol of traditional Catholicism and also as a precursor to the *Communist Manifesto*.[2] Behind all such interpretations, the question remains of just how seriously we are to take More's account. Is this really a vision of an ideal society, or simply an elaborate literary joke?

In summary, More's *Utopia* has a bipartite structure: book one contains a dialogue concerning the social ills of contemporary England, while book two describes the island of Utopia itself. This form has the effect of contrasting life in England with that of Utopia, but it remains unclear as to whether the one supports or merely undermines the other. This ambiguity is intentional, for More was understandably keen to avoid overt criticism of Tudor society at a time when such ideas, let alone their articulation in a book, would inevitably lead to a spell in the Tower. Indeed, much of *Utopia* appears to be written with a built-in defence mechanism that deflects the voice of the characters away from that of their author. So not only is the book presented as a second-hand report of the experiences of its central character, but that character, the sailor Raphael Hythloday, is given a name which, roughly translated from the Greek, means 'dispenser of nonsense.'[3]

At the start of the narrative, More is himself introduced to Hythloday by his friend Peter Giles in Antwerp, a device that once again divorces More from responsibility for the views of his character. These three characters, of whom only Hythloday is fictional, then continue, much in the manner of the classical dialogue, to debate the evils of sixteenth-century England. During these discussions Hythloday voices his disapproval of the death penalty, social inequality and unemployment, identifying the source of these ills, like Plato before him, to be private property:

> Thus I do fully persuade myself that no equal and just distribution of things can be made, nor that perfect wealth shall ever be among men, unless this propriety be exiled and banished. But so long as it shall continue, so long shall remain among the most and best part of men the heavy and inevitable burden of poverty and wretchedness. Which, as I grant that it may be somewhat eased, so I utterly deny that it can wholly be taken away.[4]

After convening for dinner, the conversation resumes with Hythloday talking of his travels as a sailor (his semifictional status is buttressed by the statement that he has sailed with Amerigo Vespucci). It is here that he embarks upon a history and description of the island of Utopia, discussing every aspect of its social and political organisation, its people, and their everyday existence. According to your point of view, More's, or rather Hythloday's, account of Utopia provides enough detail to support myriad interpretations. John Carey has provided the following summary of these opposing views:

> It is a land of happy, healthy, public-spirited communists. Money and private property are extinct. Anyone can enter any house at any time: doors are never locked. Everyone works at a trade (clothwork, masonry or carpentry) and takes a turn at agricultural labour in the countryside. Idleness is forbidden. A six-hour working day is the rule, and provides amply for everyone. Leisure is spent sensibly — attending lectures, gardening, or playing brain-stretching board games, resembling chess. There are no taverns or alehouses. Everyone goes to bed at eight o'clock.[5]

But on the other hand:

> In Utopia there is no frivolity and little freedom. Clothing is uniform, and made of undyed homespun wool. You need a permit to travel, and must go in a group. If you travel without a permit, you are arrested as a runaway and severely punished. Marital arrangements are strict and unsentimental... Adultery is punished with penal servitude. For a second offence, the penalty is death. Once a month, wives have to kneel and confess their faults to their

husbands... Each extended family, living together in a single house, is meant to have between ten and sixteen children. Any surplus children are sent to make up the tally of less prolific families. In the dining halls children wait at table or stand in respectful silence, eating only what is given them by the adult diners.[6]

From today's standpoint, those who share the view that More's society is a benevolent one are likely to find themselves in the minority. For, as always, yesterday's utopia soon becomes today's dystopia. To our minds, this particular utopia would appear to demand an unacceptable restriction of personal freedom, not to mention the familiar difficulties surrounding issues such as family life, sexuality and slavery. And yet, taken in the context of sixteenth-century England, More's contemporaries would have found much to admire here, not least those victims of religious persecution who would, no doubt, have happily gone to bed at eight in return for the religious toleration they would have been afforded. Equally, those thousands of peasants who faced starvation in Tudor England would have had little objection to the abolition of private property. And of course, More himself, sent to the Tower in 1534 and beheaded the following year, must surely have wished that he could have set sail after Hythloday, exchanging the regal tyranny of Henry VIII for the comparative security of his imaginary island.

Michel de Montaigne, *On Cannibals*

Against the backdrop of the voyages of discovery in the late fifteenth and early sixteenth centuries, utopian thinkers were finally presented with a yardstick against which to test the products of their own imaginations. The discovery of the New World provided an opportunity to judge a people free from the effects of both Christianity and civilisation, noble savages whose belief in natural law presented a challenge to the accepted practices of European society.

Michel de Montaigne (1533–92) would have known about the New World through his reading of traveller's accounts, such as Girolamo Benzoni's *Historia del Mondo Novo* (1565), and from a meeting in 1562 with three Brazilian Indians brought to France by the explorer, Nicolas Durand de Villegagnon.[7] But it wasn't until 1580 that Montaigne was to publish his first two collections of *Essais*, amongst them, 'Des Cannibales', in which he contrasts the primitive naturalism of aboriginal Indian life with what he perceives as the decadence and cynicism of sixteenth-century Europe. Montaigne's utopian essay describes an area of coastal Brazil explored by de Villegagnon in 1557 and called Antarctic France. He begins by comparing this area to Plato's account of Atlantis, lamenting that the poet could not witness such an earthly paradise for himself. For Montaigne is convinced that the inhabitants of this part of the New World are indeed living in an Eden of simplicity and abundance, free from our 'vain and frivolous enterprises.'[8] He provides the following account of daily life:

They spend the whole day dancing; the younger men go off hunting with bow and arrow. Meanwhile some of the women-folk are occupied in warming up their drink: that is their main task. In the morning, before their meal, one of the elders walks from one end of the building to the other, addressing the whole barnful of them by repeating one single phrase over and over again until he has made the rounds, their building being a good hundred yards long. He preaches two things only: bravery before their enemies and love for their wives. They never fail to stress this second duty, repeating that it is their wives who season their drink and keep it warm. [9]

Montaigne soon embarks upon a reverie of nature worship, in which these Brazilian Indians, at one with their environment, appear to act out the golden age myths of the earliest utopian dreamers. Montaigne's delight in the primitivism of these noble savages appears to know no bounds, allowing him to excuse even the least attractive trait of these wholesome people, namely their habit of eating their enemies. But is such a fate, asks Montaigne, any worse than the calculated forms of torture practised by so-called civilised Europeans? Indeed, such is their valour, that those defeated in battle would rather be killed and eaten than spared.[10]

'Des Cannibales' demonstrates the enduring appeal of the golden age myths from which all utopian literature originates. Furthermore, Montaigne's essay raised challenging questions about the ascendancy of Western civilisation at a time when new cultures were emerging which appeared to have little in common with his own. One reader who was to be heavily influenced by his account was William Shakespeare, who read John Florio's translation of the essay, published in 1603. And it is here, in *The Tempest* (1611), that Montaigne's position is encapsulated in a digression by Gonzalo, one of the Italians who find themselves shipwrecked on Prospero's island:

> I'th' commonwealth I would, by contraries,
> Execute all things; for no kind of traffic
> Would I admit; no name of magistrate;
> Letters should not be known; riches, poverty,
> And use of service, none; contract, succession,
> Bourn, bound of land, tilth, vineyard, none;
> No use of metal, corn, or wine, or oil;
> No occupation; all men idle, all;
> And women too, but innocent and pure;
> No sovereignty; ...
>
> All things in common nature should produce
> Without sweat or endeavour; treason, felony,
> Sword, pike, knife, gun, or need of any engine,
> Would I not have; but nature should bring forth,
> Of its own kind, all foison, all abundance,
> To feed my innocent people...
>
> I would with such perfection govern, sir,
> To excel the golden age.[11]

Tommaso Campanella, *City of the Sun*

Born into poverty in Calabria in 1568, Giovanni Domenico was educated by Dominican monks from an early age and, having adopted the name Father Tommaso, he began a life of devotion to the church. However, open defiance of southern Italy's Spanish rulers soon resulted in arrest, imprisonment and torture by the Inquisition. Once released, he was soon rearrested on trumped-up charges of heresy and in 1600 he was sentenced to life imprisonment. It was while manacled hand and foot in the dungeon of Castel St Elmo that Campanella began a prolific writing career that was to continue throughout his 27 years of incarceration. *La Città del Sole* or *City of the Sun,* was written in Italian, rather than the more scholarly Latin, to ensure an audience amongst the common people and, although completed in 1602, it remained unpublished until 1623.

Heavily influenced by the utopian visions of Plato and More, *City of the Sun* takes the familiar form of a dialogue, once again involving a sailor who has returned from a distant voyage. This unnamed mariner recounts his journey to the Indian Ocean where he discovers a city built with seven concentric walls, each corresponding to one of the seven planets. At the centre lies a medieval citadel, home to the city's ruler, the authoritarian philosopher Prince Hoh, or Sun, and his three acolytes Pon, Sin and Mor, who are allegorical representations of power, knowledge and love.

The walls of this city are covered with symbols and diagrams, each in turn representing a different science or art, and these walls serve to provide visual instruction to the City's inhabitants, the Solarians. The community is, unsurprisingly, a model of health, happiness and virtue. The Solarians, freed from the corrupting influence of private property, and benefiting from the wise application of eugenics and education, work a four-hour day, happy in their observance of the communal good. Central to the perpetuation of this model society is a rigorously enforced birth-control programme which uses astrological calculations to establish the optimum breeding pattern for its residents. Indeed, so heavily does Campanella's utopia rely on the efficacy of this astrologically planned reproductive system that no sexual act can be left to chance. On the contrary, all forms of casual sex are banned and even marital relations are closely monitored:

Like the ancient Greeks, they are all – male and female – naked when they take part in the sport of wrestling, so that the masters know who is, and who is not incapable of intercourse and which bodies are most suited to each other. And so, after washing themselves thoroughly, they have intercourse every third evening, and tall and beautiful women are coupled only with tall and strong men, fat women with thin men, and thin women with fat men, so as to achieve a balance... Nor do they have intercourse until after they have digested their meal, and first they say prayers. They have beautiful statues of famous men upon which the women gaze. Then they go to the window and pray to God in heaven to give them fine children. They sleep apart in different cells until the time when they have to come together, and then the mistress goes and opens the door of each cell. The time for this is determined by the Astrologer and the medical officer...[12]

Campanella's preoccupation with the mating habits of his imaginary population may be a consequence of his lengthy incarceration, for he certainly outstrips his utopian forbears Plato and More in the degree of emphasis he gives to this particular aspect of his ideal society. In other respects, however, *City of the Sun* appears to offer a careful blend of Plato's authoritarianism, More's abolition of poverty, and his contemporary, Bacon's, steadfast belief in the benefits of scientific progress. Indeed, *City of the Sun*, together with Bacon's *New Atlantis*, have been described as 'the two most science-minded utopias ever written', despite the fact that neither could have been aware of the other's work.[13] One final aspect of Campanella's work worthy of note, and one which differentiates him from his fellow utopians, is the fact that the *City of the Sun* is the first utopia to abolish slave labour. And perhaps it is this idea, rather than his most fanciful scientific speculations, that ought to be regarded as truly revolutionary.

Francis Bacon, *New Atlantis*

Like More before him, Francis Bacon was a lawyer and statesman, eventually rising to become Lord Chancellor in 1618. Also like More, he was to spend time in the Tower, where he was imprisoned briefly in 1621 after he was convicted of taking bribes. He survived this experience intact, however, and over the course of his life he produced a huge body of work, much of which was concerned with the principles of scientific inquiry. This scientific interest was complemented by an involvement with contemporary politics, and it is these two subjects which provide the basis to his utopian fable, *New Atlantis*, first published in 1627, the year after his death. The title of what was Bacon's only novel immediately returns us to the beginning of this survey and the mythical origins of utopia. Bacon draws upon Plato's discussion of Atlantis in the *Timaeus* and *Critias* in his *New Atlantis*, but this utopia is not a return to an earlier age. Instead, Bacon's novel is a futuristic fable on the benefits and dangers of science. Indeed, it has been described as the first science fiction novel and, as such, it inaugurates a tradition of utopian writing that has come to dominate the genre today.[14]

And yet, while many of the themes of his novel look to our time, the form that his utopia takes, that of an isolated Pacific island, is one that is rooted in the early modern era. Utopias of this period invariably were distanced from the outside world and were located by their authors in regions of uncharted isolation. Hence, following the example of More's *Utopia*, in which Hythloday is a sailor who has accompanied Vespucci on his voyages, Bacon's Bensalem is situated beyond the perimeter of the known world. As Susan Bruce has noted, the primary reason for this is to lend plausibility to a narrative which seeks to reveal a hitherto undiscovered society. Yet these very utopias were written against a backdrop of Renaissance exploration, the discoveries of which provided exactly the credibility that their authors sought to achieve.[15] Consequently, *New*

Atlantis begins with the line 'We sailed from Peru... for China and Japan, by the South Sea', immediately placing the reader in territory 'utterly unknown' and which might reveal 'islands or continents that hitherto were not come to light.'[16] In fact, Bacon's text reads much like a fictional travel guide in which the unnamed narrator offers the reader a detailed account of life in Bensalem, from his arrival and quarantine in the 'Strangers' House', to his meetings with Bensalem's inhabitants. The majority of the text is given over to his discussions during three such meetings, in which he is in turn informed of Bensalem's laws and history, its sexual and marital customs and, finally, the workings of its most important institution, Salomon's House. Named in honour of Bensalem's original 'lawgiver', Salomona, it is here that the narrator is informed of the scientific experiments and practices which dominate life on the island:

> We have engine-houses, where are prepared engines and instruments for all sorts of motions. There we imitate and practise to make swifter motions than any you have, either out of your muskets or any engine that you have... We represent also ordnance and instruments of war and engines of all kinds; and likewise new mixtures and compositions of gun-powder, wildfires burning in water, and unquenchable. Also fire-works of all variety both for pleasure and use. We imitate also flights of birds, we have some degrees of flying in the air; we have ships and boats for going under water, and brooking of seas... We imitate also motions of living creatures, by images of men, beasts,

birds, fishes, and serpents. We have also a great
number of other various motions, strange for equality, fineness, and subtlety.[17]

Bacon was a founding father of the scientific method that
emerged in Europe in the seventeenth and eighteenth
centuries and his utopian vision remains a remarkably
prescient one. The inhabitants of Bensalem, as John Carey
notes, have anticipated many of the scientific discoveries of
today: 'They have developed synthetic perfumes and
flavours, robots which imitate men, animals and fish,
sound-synthesizers, submarines, engines that travel faster
than a bullet, flying machines, telephones, explosives more
destructive than any available in the seventeenth century,
and something that sounds remarkably like Napalm.'[18] The
text can be taken as an illustration of just what a society can
achieve if it is grounded in a thorough understanding of
scientific methods. Indeed, with its blueprint for a model
scientific institution, New Atlantis has been credited with
providing the basis for the Royal Society which was later to
bring science to the forefront of English life.[19]

But New Atlantis remains a fable, a story with a message
that is more than simply a straightforward oration of the
blessings of scientific progress. For Bacon was alert to
contemporary fears that science might challenge the role
of Christian morality, as well as to the dangers that science
might bring if manipulated for political ends.
Consequently, the inhabitants of Bensalem remain devoutly
Christian and, crucially, its scientists retain the right to
withhold scientific knowledge from their rulers (Bensalem
is a monarchy), if it serves the wider interest of the state:

'We have consultations, which of the inventions and experiences which we have discovered shall be published, and which not: and take all an oath of secrecy, for the concealing of those which we think fit to keep secret: though some of those we do reveal sometimes to the state, and some not.'[20] Ultimately, as Bacon demonstrates, the scientific utopia, perhaps more than any other example of the genre, runs the risk of nightmarish transformation. For science and politics remain an unstable and highly toxic combination. As a result, Bacon's utopia may be read as both a celebration of scientific knowledge and as a warning of its inherent dangers.

Margaret Cavendish, *The Blazing World*

The Description of a New World Called the Blazing World (1666) by Margaret Cavendish, Duchess of Newcastle, is the first recorded English utopia by a female writer. Born to a rich family in Essex in 1623, Cavendish (née Lucas) was later to marry William Cavendish, Marquis of Newcastle, and subsequently she was to move in Royalist circles, living in exile in Antwerp during the English Civil War. It was during her time abroad that she began to write, producing a prolific stream of poetry, philosophy, political and scientific treatises, and plays. *The Blazing World* was preceded by a short utopian blueprint entitled 'The Inventory of Judgement's Commonwealth' (1655) and by the time she returned to England at the Restoration her reputation was well-founded, even though it was one of personal excess and flamboyant eccentricity. Indeed, so self-consciously idiosyncratic was Cavendish that one contemporary commentated that, 'there are many soberer people in Bedlam'. Her massive oeuvre has since been almost entirely neglected.[21] It is only in recent years, within the context of utopian and feminist writing, that Cavendish has found a new audience for her extravagant brand of fantasy.

The Blazing World is certainly unique. A mixture of romance and early science fiction, it takes on the familiar form of the imaginary voyage, in which an anonymous young lady is abducted by a foreign merchant and taken to the North Pole. Here, her captor and crew freeze to death, and the ship crosses into another world, the Blazing World, where the young lady is promptly made Empress and granted absolute power by her new husband to rule over this new land. In a moment of bizarre rebirth, the young lady is transformed into a mighty queen, a cross between Elizabeth I and Cinderella:

> Her accoutrement after she was made Empress, was as followeth: On her head she wore a cap of pearl, and a half-moon of diamonds just before it; on the top of her crown came spreading over a broad carbuncle, cut in the form of the sun; her coat was of pearl, mixt with blue diamonds, and fringed with red ones; her buskins and sandals were of green diamonds: in her left hand she held a buckler, to signify the defence of her dominions; which buckler was made of that sort of diamond as has several different colours; and being cut and made in the form of an arch, showed like a rainbow; in her right hand she carried a spear made of white diamond, cut like the tail of a blazing-star,

which signified that she was ready to assault those that proved her enemies.[22]

But the Empress of the Blazing World is not the only one to have undergone a transformation, for this world is populated by men in the shapes of bears, foxes, geese, worms, fish, flies, magpies, ants and numerous other creatures, all of whom fall under the dominion of the Emperor and his all-powerful Queen. The Blazing World is an absolute monarchy in which all government officials are castrated to make them less troublesome.[23] And, with the Emperor a largely absent figure, it is clear that it is female power that holds sway here. The plot is made even more peculiar by the introduction of Margaret Cavendish herself who appears as the Empress's scribe and with whom she begins a platonic love affair. Soon, however, the Empress learns that, in our world, her country is under attack and she returns home with her army. Using a Blazing-World chemical that ignites with water to utterly destroy every nation that will not pay allegiance to her King, she has soon granted him the same absolute world-dominion that she herself had previously enjoyed.[24]

The Blazing World appears to be a utopia that has only one inhabitant in mind, Margaret Cavendish herself. Men are either absent, castrated or transformed into animal hybrids, while the Empress is clearly a reflection of Cavendish herself, making her relationship with Cavendish's character little more than an obsessive form of self-love. In *The Blazing World*, power is virtue, and absolute power grants the freedom to transform oneself, allowing Cavendish to escape from the restrictions of seventeenth-century England and to revel in a fantasy of female domination.

Henry Neville, *The Isle of Pines*

Born in 1620, the son of a diplomat, and, like More and Bacon before him, an active figure in the politics of his day, Henry Neville was to become a member of Cromwell's Council of State. During his time in parliament he produced a number of tracts and pamphlets, amongst them *The Isle of Pines*, first published as two separate pamphlets, and first appearing in its current form in 1668. It proved highly popular, and was soon to be widely translated. Neville married but, unlike the fictional progenitor of his utopia, never had children.[25]

If Campanella's *City of the Sun* presents a society in which sexuality is strictly regulated and procreation is rigorously governed by astrological and eugenic principles, then Henry Neville's *The Isle of Pines* goes some way to reversing this scenario, offering a utopian vision of sexual abundance. Once again a travel narrative purporting to relate the 'true' account of a sailor in the South Seas, the story is narrated by the Dutch seaman, Henry Cornelius Van Sloetten, who is blown off course in a storm and finds himself at the Isle of Pines. Here, he finds an island populated by 12,000 people, all of whom descend from the Englishman George Pine, shipwrecked there with four women in 1569. The King of the Isle, George Pine's grandson William, gives Van Sloetten a copy of his grandfather's journal, which records his journey to the island and his subsequent adventures. Pine's narrative reveals an account of unbridled sexual freedom, as he, his master's fifteen-year-old daughter, two maidservants and a negro slave embark on the arduous task of populating the island:

Idleness and a fullness of everything begot in me a desire for enjoying the women. Beginning now to grow more familiar, I had persuaded the two maids to let me lie with them, which I did at first in private; but after, custom taking away shame (there being none but us), we did it more openly, as our lusts gave us liberty. Afterwards my master's daughter was content also to do as we did. The truth is, they were all handsome women, when they had clothes, and well shaped, feeding well. For we wanted no food, and living idly, and seeing us at liberty to do our wills, without hope of ever returning home made us thus bold. One of the first of my consorts, with whom I first accompanied, the tallest and handsomest, proved presently with child. The second was my master's daughter. And the other also not long after fell into the same condition, none now remaining but my negro, who seeing what we did, longed also for her share. One night, I being asleep, my negro with the consent of the others got close to me, thinking it being dark to beguile me, but I awaking and feeling her, and perceiving who it was, yet willing to try the difference, satisfied myself with her, as well as with one of the rest. That night, although the first time, she proved also with child, so that in the year of our being there, all my women were with child by me; and they all coming at different seasons, were a great help to one another.[26]

By the time of his death at the age of eighty, Pine has produced an astonishing 1,789 children, and these descendants are organised into different tribes according to the names of their respective mothers. His narrative is passed on for safe-keeping into the hands of his eldest son, who continues with his father's work, sleeping incestuously with his half-siblings in order to sustain this population-boom. In fact, there seems very little else for Pine and his descendants to do. Not only is this utopia one of sexual plenty but the natural fertility of the island precludes the need for agriculture, and there seems little need for any institutions with which to regulate this happy society.

The central role given to sex and sexuality in Neville's utopia has resulted in it receiving little serious critical attention and it has been dismissed as merely a pornotopia, a 'narrative of phallic wish-fulfilment'.[27] In support of this view, it has been noted that the name 'Pines' is an anagram of penis, while 'Sloetten' may suggest the word 'slut'.[28] And yet Pine's narrative is, literally, only half the story.

Neville first published his tale in two separate pamphlets, the first recording Pine's prolific achievements, the second telling Van Sloetten's side of the story. It was only later that Pine's narrative became framed within Sloetten's as a single text, and it appears that some readers have mistaken Pine's partial account for the whole. If so, this would indeed conform to little more than a return to an Arcadian myth, but Van Sloetten's tale is a less carefree one and recounts the community's downfall. For, entertained on the island by Pine's grandson William, Van Sloetten is told of the community's collapse following his grandfather's death, as the population 'fell to whoredoms, incests and adultery; so that what my grandfather was forced to do for necessity, they did for wantonness.'[29] Soon a range of punishments is introduced to curb such transgressions and civil war breaks out. Dutch visitors to the island are enlisted to quell this rebellion and they help to capture and kill the rebel leader before leaving the island and allowing Van Sloetten to complete his journey home. In effect, Neville's *The Isle of Pines* is two stories woven into one, a utopia that degenerates into its opposite, as an Arcadian paradise of peace and harmony fragments and falls into barbarism. In this sense, it is, perhaps, a moral tale, in which a good, but idle, society sows the seeds of its own downfall. And, if so, then it simply takes its place within a tradition of paradise lost that is itself a hallmark of utopian history. Ultimately, Neville's intentions remain unclear, and his text displays an ambivalence that resists our attempts to extract any definitive meaning. For several hundred years, Neville's tale has largely been overlooked, but perhaps the greatest legacy of *The Isle of Pines* remains its influence upon a future narrative of shipwreck that was to define the genre and to provide another, rather less hedonistic, expression of utopian ideals.

Notes

[1] Claeys and Sargent, p.77.
[2] For a detailed analysis of More's attitude to Communism see Paul Turner's appendix to his translation of *Utopia*. Thomas More, *Utopia* (1516), ed. by Paul Turner, Harmondsworth: Penguin, 1965, pp. 149–151.
[3] Turner, p. 39.

4 Thomas More, 'Utopia', trans. by Ralph Robinson, in *Three Early Modern Utopias*, ed. by Susan Bruce, Oxford: Oxford University Press, 1999, p. 45.

5 Carey, p. 38.

6 Carey, p. 39–40.

7 Carey, p. 50.

8 Michel de Montaigne, 'On Cannibals', in *Essays: A Selection*, trans. by MA Screech, London: Penguin, 1993, p. 83.

9 Montaigne, p. 85.

10 Montaigne, p. 88.

11 William Shakespeare, *The Tempest*, Act 2, Scene 1, qtd. in Claeys & Sargent, p. 106.

12 Tommaso Campanella, *The City of the Sun*, trans. by AM Elliott and R Millner, London: Journeyman Press, 1981, p. 29.

13 AL Morton, 'Introduction', Tommaso Campanella, *The City of the Sun*, trans. by AM Elliott and R Millner, London: Journeyman Press, 1981, p. 12.

14 Carey, p. 63.

15 Susan Bruce, ed., *Three Early Modern Utopias*, Introduction, p. x.

16 Francis Bacon, 'New Atlantis' in *Three Early Modern Utopias*, p. 152.

17 Bacon, 'New Atlantis', pp. 182–183.

18 Carey, p. 63.

19 Bruce, Introduction, p. xxxi.

20 Bacon, 'New Atlantis', p. 184.

21 Kate Lilley, 'Introduction', in Margaret Cavendish, *The Description of a New World Called the Blazing World and OtherWritings*, London: Pickering & Chatto, 1992, p. xiii.

[22] Margaret Cavendish, *The Description of a New World Called the Blazing World and Other Writings*, ed. by Kate Lilley, London: Pickering & Chatto, 1992, p.132.

[23] Carey, p. 78.

[24] Carey, p. 79.

[25] Carey, p. 90.

[26] Henry Neville, 'The Island of Pines', in *Three Early Modern Utopias*, ed. by Susan Bruce, Oxford: Oxford University Press, 1999, p. 198.

[27] Bruce, Introduction, p. xli.

[28] Bruce, p. xxxvii.

[29] Bruce, p. xl.

Shipwrecked:
Crusoe and the Imaginary Voyage

As eighteenth-century Europe moved inexorably towards revolution, utopian ideas could no longer be contained within imagined island communities, isolated from the political turmoil out of which they had arisen. For, as *Robinson Crusoe* was to illustrate, the further one sought to distance an imaginary community from its homeland, the more such ideal worlds came to resemble and recreate the Europe they had left behind. From Crusoe to Gulliver, from *Candide* to *Rasselas*, the imaginary voyage charted the farthest corners of the New World, only to discover images of our own society, reflected through the prism of our shared longing for personal freedom and material abundance. Soon, however, these utopian visions began to reflect a change in tone as well as content, as the travel narrative gave way to satires which were more overt in their critique of contemporary society than ever before. Utopia was increasingly defined through an absence of those inequalities and injustices which blighted the societies of these intrepid travellers as they set out in search of the ideal. And yet could such imaginary voyages ever hope to discover the perfection they sought? De Bougainville, like many before and since, believed he had located paradise in the South Seas, only to find that one could not escape the deficiencies of human nature. Could this restless search for perfection ever lead to utopia and, if we were to find it, would we wish to stay?

Daniel Defoe, *Robinson Crusoe*

Since its publication in 1719, *The Life and Strange Surprizing Adventures of Robinson Crusoe* has attained classic status, endlessly reprinted, filmed and discussed; it is seen by many as marking the starting-point of the novel in English. Indeed, so influential has this tale of shipwreck, isolation and renewal proved, that it has given its name to an entire genre of such tales, and generations of 'Robinsonades' have followed in its wake throughout world literature. Furthermore, it has provided an archetype for the concept of the imaginary voyage, the verb 'Robinsonner' (reputedly coined by Rimbaud), meaning 'to let the mind wander or to travel mentally.'[1]

The position of *Robinson Crusoe* within the utopian canon is equally groundbreaking. For, with its detailed descriptions of Crusoe's environment and his painstaking attempts to establish his own primitive society, Defoe's novel moves away from the familiar tale of lost worlds and material abundance, in favour of what reads as a factual account of human inventiveness, industry and self-improvement. In fact, *Robinson Crusoe* is grounded in the adventures of real-life castaway, Alexander Selkirk, a Scots mariner who was marooned in the South Pacific archipelago of Juan Fernández, where he survived alone for more than four years until his rescue in 1709. From the outset then, *Robinson Crusoe* is by no means a traditional utopia, in which a fully-formed society is revealed, but rather the account of one man's struggle to transform his surroundings, and in the process, himself.

The story is a familiar one, perhaps the most easily recognised in all literature. Born in York, the young Crusoe chooses to go to sea, looking for a life of adventure, and, in doing so, he rejects the advice of his father who counsels him to follow the 'middle station' in life:

> He bid me observe it, and I should always find, that the Calamities of Life were shared among the upper and the lower Part of Mankind; but that the middle Station had the fewest Disasters, and was not expos'd to so many Vicissitudes as the higher or lower Part of mankind; nay, they were not subjected to so many Distempers and Uneasinesses either of Body or Mind, as those were who, by vicious Living, Luxury and Extravagancies on one Hand, or by hard Labour, Want of Necessaries, and mean or insufficient Diet on the other Hand, bring Distempers upon themselves by the natural Consequences of their Way of Living; That the middle Station of Life was calculated for all kinds of Vertues and all kinds of Enjoyments, that Peace and Plenty were the Hand-maids of a middle Fortune; that Temperance, Moderation, Quietness, Health, Society, all agreeable Diversions, and all desirable Pleasures, were the Blessings attending the middle Station of Life; that this Way Men went silently and smoothly thro' the World and comfortably out of it, not embarrass'd with the Labours of the Hands or of the Head, not sold to the Life of Slavery for daily Bread, or harrast with perplex'd Circumstances,

which rob the Soul of Peace, and the Body of Rest; not enrag'd with the Passion of Envy, or secret burning Lust of Ambition for great things; but in easy Circumstances sliding gently thro' the World, and sensibly tasting the Sweets of living, without the bitter, feeling that they are happy, and learning by every Day's Experience to know it more sensibly.[2]

Needless to say, Crusoe's decision proves a poor one and he pays the consequences, soon finding himself shipwrecked and alone. And yet his father's advice should not be forgotten, for, in his new-found state, Crusoe endeavours to rebuild the middle-class existence he has left behind, employing the virtues of hard work and self-sufficiency that his father had instilled in him. Crusoe's island offers none of the temptations available on the *Isle of Pines*, for example. Instead, abandoned and seemingly alone, Crusoe finds himself in a state of nature, a situation in which he must overcome the obstacles of the natural world in order to survive. His subsequent experiences, as he manages to establish a degree of dominance over his surroundings, do not read like a traditional narrative of adventure but instead document in minute detail the development of his new environment, as he carefully marshals the natural resources, growing crops and constructing a home for himself. This combination of the traditional values of industriousness and inventiveness have led many to see Crusoe's tale as one of nascent capitalism, a middle-class utopia which outlines the birth and progression of 'Economic man' as he manages to gain victory over nature and to establish himself as master of his own domain. Readers such as Rousseau, Samuel Johnson, and later Karl Marx, have all seen Defoe's tale as an allegory of man's relationship to his environment, in which an initial dependency soon gives way to domination.

The purity of this solitary existence is somewhat confused by the arrival of Friday, a true native, who is rescued by Crusoe and becomes his man-servant. Friday's savagery is tamed by Crusoe, who teaches him English and Christian values, thus emphasising the superiority of civilised society over the state of nature endorsed by Montaigne, and later Rousseau. Life on Crusoe's island may provide a critique of the shortcomings of English society but Crusoe remains a product of his upbringing and, rather than starting anew, he attempts to transplant many of the conventions of his own day to his new environment. As a consequence, *Robinson Crusoe* is a highly ambiguous utopia, in which the solitary pleasures of the natural environment are repeatedly offset by cravings for material advancement. Although he has been transported to an isolated island in which he can begin again, Crusoe is unable to forget his father's admonitions and he sets about reinventing the society he has left behind. The utopian impulse at work in *Robinson Crusoe* is not, therefore, one which seeks to establish a society materially different from his own. For, having been stranded for some twenty-eight years, Crusoe's reward, and one which he never ceases to strive for, is his return home to England, where, happily, he finds himself a wealthy man. Yet, if Crusoe's utopia betrays his inability to discard the material comforts of his own society, it is also one that is underwritten by a belief in human progress and the idea of spiritual development. For

Crusoe's long isolation is characterised also by a spiritual renewal, as he embraces God and attempts to mend his ways. In this respect, *Robinson Crusoe* remains a utopia that is viewed by its principal inhabitant as a form of punishment for a misspent life, a paradox which lends Defoe's novel its unique position within the genre.

Jonathan Swift, *Gulliver's Travels*

The satirical utopia is as old as the genre itself, its primary aim being to highlight the shortcomings and absurdities of contemporary society. Its most famous exponent is Jonathan Swift, whose *Gulliver's Travels* (1726) mercilessly targets many of the political, cultural and scientific orthodoxies of his day. Published under the title, *Travels into Several Remote Nations of the World* and purporting to be written by one Lemuel Gulliver, 'First a Surgeon and then a Captain of Many Ships', Swift's satire is a parody of the emerging and hugely popular genre of the traveller's tale. His story adopts the familiar pattern of maritime voyage and subsequent shipwreck and once again targets the largely uncharted spaces of the South Pacific. And like Defoe's *Robinson Crusoe*, Swift goes to great pains to lend his work a sheen of factual accuracy, supplying an accurate geography for his fantastic adventures and using a wealth of circumstantial detail to position *Gulliver's Travels* carefully within the context of contemporary scientific and maritime accounts. As a result, several of Swift's readers took Gulliver at his word, ascribing his adventures to reality rather than fiction.

Gulliver's Travels comprises four books, each of which

corresponds to a different voyage and the discovery of new and exotic lands and their mysterious inhabitants. In the first book, he is taken prisoner by the six-inch-high Lilliputians and his observations of their court provide the basis for a satirical attack on the Court of George I. He eventually falls foul of the Lilliputians before escaping and returning to England. The second book sees this situation reversed as he finds himself in Brobdingnag, the land of the giants. Gulliver is treated as a curiosity and exhibited for money before being bought by the Queen and taken to Court. Here he discusses the state of Europe with the King, who remains unimpressed. Book three takes Gulliver to the floating island of Laputa, whose population devote themselves to music and mathematics, becoming so preoccupied by these that they are in constant danger of collision. Once again, Gulliver escapes to England, but he returns to sea once more in book four, 'A Voyage to the Country of the Houyhnhnms', and it is in this final section that Swift provides his image of utopia.

Living on an island, free from human vices, the Houyhnhnms are horses. Yet these horses have organised a society far superior to our own, their natural virtue and emphasis upon reason allowing them to establish a rational community untroubled by the illogical emotions and dangerous passions that characterise human life. This is a society that cannot but compare favourably with Gulliver's, a fact that he demonstrates by listing those aspects of eighteenth-century England that are happily absent from the land of the Houyhnhnms:

Here were no Gibers, Censurers, Backbiters, Pickpockets, Highwaymen, House-breakers, Attorneys, Bawds, Buffoons, Gamesters, Politicians, Wits, Spleneticks, tedious Talkers, Controvertists, Ravishers, Murderers, Robbers, Virtuosos; no Leaders of Followers of Party or Faction; no Encouragers to Vice, by Seducement or Examples: No Dungeon, Axes, Gibbets, Whipping-posts, or Pillories; No cheating Shopkeepers or Mechanicks: No Pride, Vanity or Affectation: No Fops, Bullies, Drunkards, strolling Whores, or Poxes: No ranting, lewd, expensive Wives: No stupid, proud Pedants: No importunate, over-bearing, quarrelsome, noisy, roaring, empty, conceited, swearing Companions: No scoundrels raised from the Dust upon the Merit of their Vices; No Lords, Fidlers, Judges or Dancing-masters. [3]

Sadly, however, this wise equine race shares its island with its much less appealing neighbours, the vicious, greedy, and repulsive Yahoos. Used by the Houyhnhnms for menial work, the Yahoos, who closely resemble humans, live in a state of nature but have little in common with the noble savage of Montaigne or Rousseau. Instead, these creatures reveal Swift's rather depressing view of human nature, one of essential brutishness and irredeemable stupidity:

Their Heads and Breasts were covered with thick Hair, some frizzled and others lank, they had Beards like Goats, and a long ridge of Hair down their Backs, and the fore-parts of their Legs and Feet, but the rest of their Bodies were bare, so that I might see their Skins, which were of a brown buff Colour. They had no Tails, nor any Hair at all on their Buttocks, except about the *Anus*... Upon the whole, I never beheld in all my Travels so disagreeable an Animal... A Herd of at least forty came flocking about me from the next Field, houling and making odious Faces... Several of this cursed Brood getting hold of the Branches behind leaped up in the Tree, from whence they began to discharge their Excrements on my Head...[4]

Not surprisingly, after this initial encounter, Gulliver rejects the companionship of the Yahoos in favour of life as a member of the Houyhnhnms' household. He develops an admiration for their lifestyle which he begins to emulate. But, unfortunately for Gulliver, he cannot wholly cast off his Yahoo roots and, despite his apparent rationality, he is eventually expelled from the Houyhnhnm community. Having found his way home to England, however, Gulliver discovers that he can no longer abide the company of other humans, his family included, and he seeks refuge in his horses' stables.

In many ways, Gulliver's depiction of the Land of the Houyhnhnms resembles Hythloday's account of Utopia in More's text, but there is one crucial difference. For, while Hythloday finds a home in his utopia, where he lives happily for five years, Gulliver is never accepted by his hosts and is ultimately banished. Gulliver finds his ideal society only to discover that he is not welcome there and, for this reason, *Gulliver's Travels* sits uncomfortably within the utopian tradition. On the one hand, it imagines an ideal society but on the other, it displays the belief that humanity is unworthy of entry to such a place. Swift's satire undercuts the very possibility of an ideal world, for us at least, and, in challenging the very idea of human perfectibility, *Gulliver's Travels* marks a turning point in the history of utopia. In denying us the possibility of such a world, the idealistic impulse of so much utopian writing is challenged and rerouted, as a more sceptical and less optimistic outlook emerges in its place.

Voltaire, *Candide*

The most famous opponent of the belief that all is for the best, in this, the best of all possible worlds, is Voltaire who satirises such a position in *Candide* (1758). It was the philosophy of Optimism which proclaimed that it was only the limitations of human understanding that prevented us from recognising our own world as the utopia we had been seeking in vain elsewhere. Principally associated with the German philosopher Gottfried Leibniz, such a belief was also propagated by the poet Alexander Pope, who confidently asserted:

> All Nature is but art, unknown to thee;
> All chance, direction which thou canst not see;
> All discord, harmony not understood;
> All partial evil universal good:
> And spite of pride, in erring reason's spite,
> One truth is clear, Whatever is, is RIGHT.[5]

A satirical successor to *Gulliver's Travels*, Voltaire's novella has a picaresque and fast moving plot which parodies the

traveller's tale while giving voice to a succession of philosophical asides. The mouthpiece for the philosophy of optimism is provided by Dr Pangloss, family tutor to the young
Candide. Over the course of some thirty episodic chapters, the strength of his conviction is tested to the full, as
he and Candide, now penniless and exiled from their home
in Westphalia, find themselves experiencing an extraordinary array of mishaps and disasters. Having survived the
Lisbon Earthquake of 1755, not to mention the Portuguese
Inquisition, shipwreck, flogging and hanging, the pair
journey around the globe, travelling from one calamity to
the next. Eventually, however, and in Pangloss's absence,
Candide and his servant, Cacambo, find themselves sailing
down a river in the New World, and it is here that they
discover the land of El Dorado:

> He and Cacambo stepped ashore at the first village
> they came to. A few village children, covered in
> tattered gold brocade, were playing quoits at the
> entrance to the settlement. Our two men from the
> other world stopped to watch them. Their quoits
> were fairly large, round objects, some of them yellow,
> some red, some green, and they gleamed in an odd
> way. The travellers were prompted to pick some of
> them up. They were pieces of gold, emerald, and
> ruby, and the smallest of them would have been the
> greatest ornament on the Mogul's throne.[6]

This vision of El Dorado is Voltaire's utopia, a magical
country of material abundance where all men are free,
there are no jails or courts, and, in a society in which

monetary value has no meaning, children play in the streets with gold and precious stones. Sheltered from the greed and corruption of European society, the citizens of El Dorado have pledged never to leave, remaining in happy isolation within their ideal kingdom. After a month in El Dorado, however, perfection begins to pall and Candide decides to leave in search of Cunégonde, the woman he hopes to marry. Despite the advice of the King, who warns them against leaving, they make their way, now fabulously wealthy, back to the world they had left behind. Naturally enough, they quickly lose all their money and are returned to a cycle of misfortune and calamity. They soon acquire a new companion, Martin, who, by challenging the optimistic philosophy of Pangloss, and voicing the beliefs of Voltaire himself, begins to persuade Candide that human nature is not quite as he had been led to believe:

'Do you think,' said Candide, 'that men have always massacred each other the way they do now? that they've always been liars, cheats, traitors, ingrates, brigands? that they've always been feeble, fickle, envious, gluttonous, drunken, avaricious, ambitious, blood-thirsty, slanderous, debauched, fanatical, hypercritical, and stupid?'

'Do you think,' said Martin, 'that hawks have always eaten pigeons when they find them?'

'Yes, no doubt,' said Candide.

'Well, then', said Martin, 'if hawks have always had the same character, why do you expect men to have changed theirs?'[7]

In depicting utopia as a place in which human dissatisfaction remains, a place which Candide leaves voluntarily,
Voltaire questions the very possibility of an ideal world,
suggesting that such a place runs contrary to human nature
and the perpetual longing for change. Contentment and
complete happiness are chimeras for Voltaire, mere illu-
sions which force one onward towards an imaginary destination that has never existed. This point is repeated
throughout *Candide*, most notably in the passage in which
Candide is finally reunited with Cunégonde. For, by now,
she has grown hideously ugly and Candide only marries her
out of spite for her brother. His long journey and the
repeated hardships he has experienced have ultimately
been in vain, a purposelessness which is simply the defin-
ing characteristic of the human condition. The conclusion
of the novel sees Candide finally dismiss his tutor's optimistic philosophy, in favour of the rather enigmatic belief
that 'we must cultivate our garden.'[8] This passage has been
subjected to endless academic scrutiny, but Voltaire's
message appears to suggest that one must choose the
simple life, if one is to successfully keep at bay the three
great evils of human existence, 'boredom, vice and need.'[9]
In this respect, the life of the gardener, cultivating his land,
is infinitely superior to an existence devoted to intellectual
pursuits, and each of us must tend to our own 'garden' if
we are to have any hope of contentment.

Samuel Johnson, *Rasselas*

Ye who listen with credulity to the whispers of fancy,
and pursue with eagerness the phantoms of hope;

who expect that age will perform the promises of youth, and that the deficiencies of the present day will be supplied by the morrow; attend to the history of Rasselas prince of Abissinia.[10]

Published just a few weeks after *Candide*, and resembling Voltaire's book both in its satirical tone and in its scepticism towards human perfectibility, Johnson's *The History of Rasselas, Prince of Abissinia* was reputed to have been completed in a week in order to raise funds to cover his mother's funeral expenses. Certainly, *Rasselas* offers a pragmatic counterblast to the more fanciful examples of utopianism and, in sounding a note of caution to those valuing hope over experience, it has been described as 'perhaps the wisest book ever written.'[11]

Johnson's evident reservations towards those accounts which, in claiming to offer factual descriptions of newly discovered realms, instead merely relay the imaginary excesses of their authors, can be seen in his translation of the Jesuit Father Jeronymo Lobo's *Voyage to Abyssinia*, published some 24 years before *Rasselas*, in 1735. Here, in his preface to this work, Johnson notes with evident approval that Lobo appears to have 'consulted his senses, not his imagination', in producing a work free from the 'romantic absurdities or incredible fictions' to be found elsewhere: 'The reader will here find no regions cursed with irremediable barrenness, or blest with spontaneous fecundity; no perpetual gloom, or unceasing sunshine; nor are the nations here described either devoid of all sense of humanity, or consummate in all private and social virtues...'[12]

In privileging knowledge over the imagination, the reader might expect *Rasselas* to display an anti-utopian spirit of rationalism, but instead Johnson's book remains a much less straightforward blend of satire, comedy and philosophy; not so much anti-utopian, as a reverse utopia, in which his protagonist, Prince Rasselas, struggles to escape from his confinement within the oppressive perfection of the Happy Valley. For this world of seeming bliss and contentment displays the paradox of utopianism: how can one ever know happiness if one has never experienced its opposite? This is the conundrum that Rasselas faces because, uniquely within his community, he comes to question the bland perfection of his world, eager to measure his own experiences against those whose lives are less fortunate than his own. From the outset then, the Happy Valley appears as a kind of Eden, and Rasselas as a dissatisfied Adam.[13] And it is from this earthly paradise that Rasselas and a few companions escape in search of worldly misery and the true meaning of happiness. This search takes them to Egypt, and it is here that they experience a series of adventures which help to resolve this quest. Along the way Rasselas is used by Johnson as a mouthpiece for a series of disquisitions on the good life, amongst others, the role of scientific progress, the value of travel, the benefits and disadvantages of marriage and celibacy, and the true nature of madness. Ultimately, these questions go unresolved and *Rasselas* concludes with his decision to return, albeit a changed man, to Abissinia.

Throughout this loosely connected series of arguments and events, *Rasselas* revolves around a central theme of human dissatisfaction and a hunger for new experience.[14]

For, in short, the human condition is essentially at odds with the utopian impulse, the one forever in search of novelty to alleviate the boredom of everyday existence, the other attempting to create a society in which such a search is no longer necessary. *Rasselas* presents the argument that nowhere is man truly happy, for experience is always partial and a utopian society can never bridge the gap between imagination and reality.

Louis Antoine de Bougainville,
Voyage Around the World

When Samuel Johnson railed against overblown accounts of newfound utopias, then Louis Antoine de Bougainville's description of his voyages must have been exactly the kind of work Johnson had in mind. For here we find an example of how a first-hand factual account can reveal the dreams of a Europe besotted by the idea of the South Seas.

Louis Antoine, Comte de Bougainville, was the commander of the two ships to make the first French circumnavigation of the world, and his account of this voyage, first published in French in 1771, was to identify Tahiti as the utopian capital of the world. Bougainville first sighted the island in 1768 and from the outset his journal reveals a sense of unreality, as fact and fiction collide:

> I have often, in company with only one or two of our people, been out walking in the interior parts of the isle. I thought I was transported into the Garden of Eden. We crossed a turf, covered with fine fruit trees, and intersected by little rivulets, which keep up a

pleasant coolness in the air, without any of those inconveniences which humidity occasions. A numerous people there enjoy the blessings which nature showers literally down upon them. We found companies of men and women sitting under the shade of their fruit-trees. They all greeted us with signs of friendship. Those who met us upon the road stood aside to let us pass by. Everywhere we found hospitality, ease, innocent joy, and every appearance of happiness amongst them...[15]

Despite his attempts to maintain a cool-headed factual account, Bougainville is unable to downplay the welcome of the Tahitian women whose charms colour his entire perception of the island. And yet this Eden is not the paradise it appears, for some weeks after leaving the island, Bougainville was to discover that several members of his crew had been afflicted with venereal disease. Falling back upon traditional European enmities, he laid the blame for this outbreak upon British sailors who had visited the island previously.[16] Bougainville's first impressions of Tahiti are overlaid by a European sensibility and a belief in the Golden Age that characterised early utopian dreams. But for Bougainville, this is no myth, but the real thing: 'Tahiti is no utopia, no "not place", but the real "beautiful place": "la veritable Eutopie."'[17]

Bougainville's journal has proved of greater merit as a literary endeavour than as a contribution to science. But, in many ways, his *Voyage Around the World* provides a contradictory image of Tahiti, at first presenting an idyllic image of a utopian society, before subsequently revealing a more

realistic description that bears little relationship to this
first impression. These two Tahitis sit uncomfortably within
the pages of his journal, 'the one literary and mythic and
the other ethnographic and scientific.'[18] The latter is based
upon the information provided by the Tahitian, Aotourou,
who accompanied Bougainville and his crew on their
return to France, where he was fêted as a living example of
Montaigne's innocent savage. But a Tahitian's own account
of his less than paradisiacal existence could never hope to
match the mythical force of European utopianism, and his
contribution to the journal has been entirely disregarded in
favour of Bougainville's initial impression of Tahiti as 'the
land of Venus reborn', a prelapsarian paradise of free love
amidst the palm trees.[19]

Picking up where Bougainville left off, Denis Diderot
(1713–84) was to reinforce the identification of Tahiti as
paradise on earth in his *Supplement to Bougainville's Voyage*
(1796). Revelling in the depiction of Tahitians as sexually
free natives liberated from the repressive constraints of
'civilised' values, Diderot portrayed a society tainted by its
contact with corrupt Europeans, helping to cement a myth
of an idealised community which has never fully been over-
turned. More than two hundred years later, Tahiti and her
surrounding islands have been unable to escape this
prolonged utopian longing, acquiring a parallel existence
in a plethora of excited fictional portrayals, from Melville
and Stevenson, to Pierre Loti and Somerset Maugham. And
regardless of the reality of Polynesian life in the twenty-
first century, for many Tahiti continues to symbolise an
ideal society awaiting rediscovery.

Notes

1 John Sturrock, *Céline: Journey to the End of the Night*, Cambridge: Cambridge University Press, 1990, p. 37. For an examination of the role of *Robinson* as a symbol of the wanderer in literature, see Merlin Coverley, *Psychogeography*, Harpenden: Pocket Essentials, 2006, p. 66–72.

2 Daniel Defoe, *Robinson Crusoe* (1719), ed. by Thomas Keymer, Oxford: Oxford University Press, 2007, p. 6.

3 Jonathan Swift, *Gulliver's Travels*, ed. by Claude Rawson, Oxford: Oxford University Press, 2005, p. 258.

4 Jonathan Swift, *Gulliver's Travels*, p. 209.

5 Alexander Pope, 'An Essay on Man' (1732), in *The Norton Anthology of English Literature* (Fifth Edition, Volume 1), ed. by MH Abrams, New York: Norton, 1986, p. 2270.

6 Voltaire, *Candide and Other Stories*, trans. by Roger Pearson, Oxford: Oxford University Press, 2008, p. 40.

7 Voltaire, *Candide*, p. 55.

8 Voltaire, *Candide*, p. 88.

9 Voltaire, *Candide*, p. 87.

10 Samuel Johnson, *The History of Rasselas, Prince of Abissinia*, ed. by DJ Enright, London: Penguin, 1976, p. 39.

11 Carey, p. 150.

12 Samuel Johnson, *Voyage to Abyssinia* (1735), qtd. in Enright, ed., *Rasselas*, p. 11.

13 DJ Enright, *Rasselas*, 'Introduction', p. 14.

14 DJ Enright, *Rasselas*, 'Introduction', p. 27.

15 Louis Antoine, Comte de Bougainville, *A Voyage Round the World. Performed by Order of his Most Christian Majesty, in the*

Years 1766, 1767, 1768 and 1769 (1772), trans. by John Reinhold Forster and qtd. in Carey, p. 155.

[16] Neil Rennie, *Far-Fetched Facts: The Literature of Travel and the Idea of the South Seas*, Oxford: Oxford University Press, 1995, p. 89.

[17] Rennie, p. 89.

[18] Rennie, p. 118.

[19] Rennie, p. 118.

Socialism and Utopia

Against the backdrop of American Independence and the growth of revolutionary movements across Europe, the nineteenth century saw an increasing emphasis upon human rights, equality and democracy. Utopian literature was to reflect this cultural shift as experimental communities inspired by visions of a more just and equitable society began to appear across Europe and North America. At the forefront of this desire for radical change were those figures later to be collectively labelled the Utopian Socialists. Claude-Henri de Saint Simon, Charles Fourier and Robert Owen offered markedly different solutions to the social problems of their day and expressed themselves in quite different fashions, but they shared an unwavering belief both in the necessity for social change and, crucially, in the practical implementation of their ideas. In their wake followed Marx and Engels, dismissive of their forbears' reluctance to enforce change through revolution, yet unable to recognise the utopian character of their own proposals. Finally, towards the end of the century, the form in which these ideas were presented began to move from the pamphlet and the manifesto to the novel, as Edward Bellamy and William Morris offered their own opposing visions of a future socialist society. Political ideology had found the perfect vehicle for the delineation of the future, and for much of the nineteenth century at least, this depiction was underwritten by a passionate belief in human progress.

Claude-Henri de Saint-Simon

Largely overlooked during his lifetime, Claude-Henri de Saint Simon (1760–1825) has since been recognised as both a prophetic advocate of industrial progress and an influential precursor to Socialism. Much of this legacy results from the work of his enthusiastic followers, the Saint-Simonians, who following their master's death proclaimed the advent of the New Age; establishing a number of religious cults, they were to preach a range of unorthodox doctrines, emphasising the benefits of industrialism alongside those of sexual liberation.

Unlike his fellow Utopian Socialists, Owen and Fourier, Saint-Simon had little direct experience of the realities of industrial life. Born into an aristocratic family, he was soon to become an advocate of Enlightenment thinking, abandoning religious convention for the principles of science and rationality. As a soldier, he fought in the American War of Independence and at the onset of the French Revolution he renounced his title, becoming a Republican. Over the course of the next twenty years, Saint-Simon wrote prolifically, early works in praise of the physical sciences gradually giving way to expressions of a more overtly political nature. *L'Industrie* (1817) was to establish his socialist credentials. But it was in the periodical *L'Organisateur* (1819) that he was to outline his distinction between the 'drones', the aristocracy, clergy and other idle rich, on the one hand, and the 'industrials', those employed in useful labour, on the other. Having categorised the royal family amongst the former, Saint-Simon was imprisoned on charges of subversion, only to be later acquitted. But Saint-Simon was to maintain his belief that the nobility was simply a parasitic anachronism, an outmoded form of historical development which was no longer necessary. In Saint-Simon's vision of a new world order, this redundant sector of society would be replaced by a technocratic elite who would apply the principles of science and industry for the benefit of society as a whole. These 'savants' would replace the priesthood in establishing a new religion in which the tenets of intellect and creativity would replace those of theology, while the 'industrials' would ensure the eradication of poverty and the creation of a well-educated and usefully employed workforce. The reorganisation of society and the balance of power between these two ruling classes was meticulously described, and in his *Sketch of a New Political System* (1819), Saint-Simon details his plans for a new parliament. Alongside these ideas he also reveals a brief glimpse of this utopian future, which, rather surprisingly, appears to resemble not so much an industrialised France, as a pastoral England:

The whole of French soil should be turned into a superb English park, adorned with all that the fine arts can add to the beauties of nature. For a long time luxury has been concentrated in the palaces of kings, the residences of princes, the mansions and châteaux of a few powerful men. This concentration is most detrimental to the general interests of society, because it tends to establish two different grades of civilisation, one for persons whose intelligence is developed through habitual viewing of productions of the fine arts, and one for men whose imaginative faculties undergo no development, since the material work in which they are engaged does not stimulate the intelligence.[1]

An ardent Anglophile, Saint-Simon's approval of all things English would have elicited little support in the immediate aftermath of Waterloo, and he appears to have further alienated his countrymen with his suggestion that, as a preliminary move towards European unification, England and France should unite.[2] Needless to say, Saint-Simon's notion of a peace-loving world, united by a shared faith in the progressive power of industrialism, brought him little acclaim, and depressed by this failure, he attempted suicide in 1823, managing to fire seven bullets into his head. He survived, minus an eye, only to die of gastro-enteritis two years later.

The idea that the workers could happily coexist with their enlightened bosses in a society that benefited all was seen by Marx and Engels as hopelessly idealistic, and they were to label Saint-Simon utopian as a result. And yet, the Saint-Simonian Movement flourished after his death and his steadfast belief that all men, the working classes included, could progress and benefit from industrialism was to become a hallmark of later socialist thought. Saint-Simon's attempts to establish industrialism as a religion were propounded in his most influential work, *The New*

Christianity (1825), a text vague enough to permit myriad interpretations. It is this ability to read into Saint-Simon's work any number of divergent positions that gave him his posthumous influence. For, unlike the vast majority of his utopian predecessors (but, as we shall see, in the manner of many of his fellow utopian socialists), Saint-Simon inspired his followers to actually put his ideas into practice. The most notable of these attempts was the school established by his two disciples, Barthélemy Prosper Enfantin and Amand Bazard, who were responsible for introducing the critique of private property with which Saint-Simon was later to be credited. Enfantin and Bazard were soon to fall out, however, and Enfantin went on to establish his own community in which a faith in industrialism was soon to give way to a more popular blend of mysticism, bizarre ritual and, of course, orgiastic sexual freedom. And, in this respect, he was to set the standard, in the popular imagination at least, by which many such sects were subsequently to be viewed.

Charles Fourier and the Phalanstery

Like Saint-Simon, Charles Fourier (1772–1837) has also been labelled a utopian socialist. Indeed, in the derogatory sense that Marx intended, he is one of the most utopian of writers, socialist or otherwise, in as far as his plans for a future society deviate so profoundly from what might be considered practical or even possible, yet are pursued with the zeal of the religious fanatic. In many ways, he represents the polar opposite to Saint-Simon: the former was an Anglophile whose utopia resembled the English countryside, while Fourier detested the English, regarding them as the founders of Industrialism; Saint-Simon preached a gospel of industrial progress, while Fourier was essentially a romantic, who regarded industrialism as an aberration, and an assault on human nature; Saint-Simon was, or at least regarded himself as, a rationalist, and was a fervent believer in the Enlightenment; Fourier, on the other hand, rejected the Enlightenment belief in the primacy of reason in favour of a worldview ruled by passion and emotion. What he and Saint-Simon had in common, however, was an ability to inspire their followers with an unswerving faith in the truth of their beliefs. For Fourier's writings have proven hugely influential on writers as diverse as Marx, Freud and Dostoyevsky, while communities across North America and elsewhere have sought to put his principles into practice.

Born in Besançon, France in 1772, the son of a cloth-merchant, Fourier was later employed in a series of unsat-isfying jobs that did little to dissuade him of the degrading nature of working life. Indeed, by all accounts, his was a mundane and isolated existence, his only solace being the pursuit of his utopian project which was, by contrast with his own experiences, one of unparalleled grandiosity. Fourier believed that poverty was the principal cause of society's ills, and he expressed solidarity not only with the working poor, but also with the plight of women, whom he believed to be enslaved within the confines of traditional marriage. He is credited with originating the term *féminisme* in 1837.[3] These principles were articulated through the creation of his utopian realm, Harmony.

Harmony was built upon a single, overriding proposi-tion, that human affairs are governed by a law of passionate attraction. For, just as Newton had formulated the theory of gravitational attraction, Fourier contended that human behaviour could be regulated through an understanding of the ways in which each person is attracted to certain personality types, and correspondingly certain types of activities. Fourier's 'science' of passionate attraction was calculated meticulously: there are precisely 810 different psychological types, each containing twelve fundamental passions. Multiplied by two, to account for the two genders, this figure rises to 1,620. These figures are significant, for this number, 1,620, becomes in Fourier's schema the optimum population for his ideal community. The name of this group, a perfect cross-section of human psychology and the building block of his utopian vision, was the Phalanx, and the site housing them was to be called the Phalanstery. These Phalansteries, which Fourier hoped would one day number six million, were a combination of luxury hotel and modern day shopping-mall, providing an elegant setting in which to engage in a harmonious existence of work, education and casual sex. New arrivals to these communities would be greeted with the warmest of welcomes:

The band of adventurers moves forward through a cloud of perfume and a rain of flowers. The choral groups and musicians of the Phalanx welcome them with hymns of joy. As soon as the visitors have reached the colonnades of the Phalanstery, bowls of flaming punch are brought in and a hundred different nectars spurt from the opened fountains. All the knights and ladies are wearing their most seductive clothing. Two

hundred priests and priestesses, who are dressed no
less elegantly, greet their guests and perform the
introductions. After refreshments have been served,
the whole group mounts to the throne room where
the Pontiff Isis is seated. The welcoming ceremonies
are concluded there and, after washing, all the visitors
proceed to the confessional... While the visitors are
eating a light snack, the work of analysing and classi-
fying their confessions goes on in the consistory. A list
of five or six sympathetic relationships is drawn up for
each knight and lady on the basis of the examinations
conducted by the young priests and priestesses who
wish to become sympathetic with the adventurers.
Before the snack is over the fairies and genies have
completed their task of match-making. Their recom-
mendations are delivered to the office of the High
Matron along with a summary of each confession.
Sympathetic matching takes everything into account,
and the final choices made are those which seem most
likely to complement previous encounters either
through contrast or identity.[4]

Life in the Phalanstery was not based upon equality. Work
was distributed according to the interests and desires of the
individual and wealth was determined accordingly; those
jobs that the worker did not enjoy would receive higher
pay. Similarly, just as suitable employment would be
assessed according to psychological profile, so too would
sexual relations be organised on the same basis. Fourier
recognised no boundaries when it came to sexual gratification, and all tastes were to be catered for. Matchmaking

was to be conducted by a kind of sexual priesthood who would attempt to meet the varying needs of the populace, ensuring that even the less attractive received their 'sexual minimum'. [5]

Fourier's utopian vision is undeniably eccentric, combining progressive views on social and gender relations with a highly individual philosophy of physical and psychological attraction. But this is just the start. For Fourier's clear fondness for mathematical precision was to lead him to make some truly bizarre predictions: his utopian world would last some 80,000 years; six moons would orbit the Earth; our world was only one of God's 18 creations, and so it goes on. Elsewhere, he predicts that the North Pole would become warmer than the Mediterranean, while, most famously, he was to suggest that the seas would turn into lemonade. Fourier believed that his law of passionate attraction was applicable not only to humans, but also to vegetable and mineral 'life', and he was consistent in following his principles wherever they led him, however fantastic the conclusion. As a result, Fourier's contribution to early socialist thought and his insight into human psychology have become completely overshadowed by the unbridled lunacy of his more outlandish predictions. And yet, remarkably, instead of the derision and dismissal that one might expect Fourier's work to have attracted, his utopia has proved the most widely influential of all the utopian socialists. In North America alone, experimental communities such as Brook Farm, the North American Phalanx in New Jersey and, most notably, Utopia, Ohio, were all inspired by Fourier's ideas. Not surprisingly, none of these communities was able to implement successfully the plan that Fourier had outlined. But their very existence is a testament to the enduring appeal of his vision and the power of utopian thinking in offering both a critique of society's failings and a reflection of its latent desires.

Robert Owen, *A New View of Society*

Unlike almost all his utopian predecessors, Robert Owen practised what he preached, becoming both a pioneering social reformer and a highly successful entrepreneur. Born in Newtown, Wales, the son of a saddler and ironmonger, Robert Owen (1771–1858) was a remarkably precocious child who combined a keen intellect with outstanding business acumen. As a result, having been apprenticed to a draper at the age of 11, he was running his own business by the age of 20 and was soon managing a Manchester textile mill employing 500 people. In 1799, he acquired cotton-mills at New Lanark, Scotland. It was here that he began to implement the innovative schemes of factory management which were to make New Lanark a highly-profitable business as well as a symbol for progressive and benevolent employment practices.

An opponent of the modern factory system, Owen believed that it encouraged a heartless individualism that did nothing to benefit or develop the lives of the workers. In New Lanark, Owen introduced revolutionary measures, such as shorter working hours, safer working conditions, improved housing and, most significantly, a system of education for employees and their families. For at the heart of Owen's outlook was a belief that human nature was essentially malleable and that, through the correct upbringing and training, good character could be nurtured. It was, therefore, illogical to hold individuals responsible for their opinions and actions, for human behaviour was simply the manifestation of the education that a person had received. This theory of 'philosophical necessitarianism' was at odds with the idea of man's free will, and was summarised in Owen's oft-repeated mantra, 'The character of man is formed for him, and not by him.'[6] This is a radical proposition which is, of course, in conflict with Christian notions of original sin, and Owen was to discard Christianity whilst maintaining a belief in the perfectibility of human nature. It was in his account of the formation of New Lanark in *A New View of Society, Or, Essays on the Principle of the Formation of the Human Character, and the Application of the Principle to Practice* (1813) that these ideas were first expressed:

> Let it not, therefore, be longer said that evil or injurious actions cannot be prevented, or that the most rational habits in the rising generation cannot be universally formed. In those characters which now exhibit crime, the fault is obviously not in the individual, but the defects proceed from the system in which the individual was trained. Withdraw those circumstances which tend to create crime in the human character, and crime will not be created. Replace them with such as are calculated to form habits of order, regularity, temperance, industry; and these qualities will be formed... Proceed systematically on principles of undeviating persevering kindness, yet retaining and using, with the least possible

severity, the means of restraining crime from immediately injuring society; and by degrees even the crimes now existing in the adults will also gradually disappear: for the worst formed disposition, short of incurable insanity, will not long resist a firm, determined, well-directed, persevering kindness. Such a proceeding, whenever practised, will be found the most powerful and effective corrector of crime, and of all injurious and improper habits.[7]

Following his beliefs to their logical conclusion, Owen maintained that those defects, which would previously have been viewed as the consequence of poor character, were simply the result of inadequate education and could yet be eradicated. For once man had been trained to overcome his limitations, society could itself attain perfection: 'On the experience of a life devoted to the subject, I hesitate not to say, that the members of any community may by degrees be trained to live *without idleness, without poverty, without crime, and without punishment*; for each of these is the effect of error in the various systems prevalent throughout the world. *They are all necessary consequences of ignorance.*'[8]

In Owen's view, the best way to establish such a utopian society was not through the increased productivity of the free market, but rather through increased cooperation. Owen was never to countenance the overthrow of the ruling class that Marx was later to suggest, but he is said to have first propounded the term 'Socialism', to describe a more equitable relationship between employer and worker, characterised both by a strong social conscience and a sense of communal endeavour.

Between 1805 and 1815, Owen attracted some 15,000 visitors to New Lanark and yet, despite its profitability and his own increasing fame, he was unable to encourage similar enterprises elsewhere. As hostility to his ideas grew from both his fellow industrialists and the clergy, so his beliefs hardened and he began to develop a more radical position, attacking both the concept of private property and the profit-motive itself. Soon he was calling for the establishment of a 'New Moral World' in which humanity would live in small, predominantly agricultural communities called Villages of Cooperation. Here, money would be abolished in favour of a system of 'labour notes' which could then be exchanged for goods.

Having grown frustrated by the resistance that his ideas met with in England and having failed to secure a seat in Parliament, Owen and his family left for the USA in 1824. It was here that he was to purchase some 20,000 acres of land in New Harmony, Indiana, and to establish the first and most famous of sixteen Owenite communities which were to appear in the USA between 1825 and 1829. New Harmony was not a success, however, and collapsed after his business partner ran off with the profits. Similar communities were equally short-lived and Owen returned to England in 1829, having spent a sizeable proportion of his personal wealth on his ill-fated utopian adventure. By this stage, Owen had also lost his partnership in the New Lanark mills, and for the remainder of his life, his reputation now somewhat reduced, he was to energetically continue his involvement in the cooperative movement. In 1835, he established the Rational Society which agitated for the implementation of socialist ideas. The movement attracted an enormous following with many thousands attending its series of lectures at Owenite branches, amongst them a young German factory-owner named Friedrich Engels.[9]

Karl Marx and Friedrich Engels,
The Communist Manifesto

The attitude of Marx and Engels towards utopianism was one of clearly stated antipathy. They attached some value to Utopian Socialism in its critique of capitalism and in the role that it played in rousing the proletariat towards an awareness of its own exploitation. But in favouring individual solutions rather than emphasising a historically determined class struggle, utopian thought was regarded ultimately as little more than fantasy. Despite this dismissal, however, Marx and Engels are themselves now standard entries within any overview of the utopian genre.

The most accessible, mercifully brief and, as a result, widely-read of Marx and Engels' works, *The Communist Manifesto* (1848), is also the text which engages the most directly with their utopian forbears. It is here that Marx attempts to distance himself from Saint-Simon, Fourier and Owen. For while these and others were, according to Marx, experimenting with their small and isolated communities, only he was able to comprehend the historical forces that underpinned all human relations. These nascent socialists dreamt of utopia, but lacked the insight necessary to make it a reality:

Such fantastic pictures of future society, painted at a time when the proletariat is still in a very undeveloped state and has but a fantastic conception of its own position correspond with the first instinctive yearnings of that class for a general reconstruction of society... In proportion as the modern class struggle develops and takes definite shape, this fantastic standing apart from the contest, these fantastic attacks on it, lose all practical value and all theoretical justification. Therefore, although the originators of these systems were, in many respects, revolutionary, their disciples have, in every case, formed mere reactionary sects. They hold fast by the original views of their masters, in opposition to the progressive historical development of the proletariat. They, therefore, endeavour, and that consistently, to deaden the class struggle and to reconcile the class antagonisms. They still dream of experimental realization of their social Utopias, of founding isolated 'phalanstères', of establishing 'home colonies'... and to realize all these castles in the air, they are compelled to appeal to the feelings and purses of the bourgeois. By degrees they sink into the category of reactionary conservative Socialists... differing from these only by more systematic pedantry, and by their fanatical and superstitious belief in the miraculous effects of their social science.[10]

By labelling these early socialist thinkers as utopian, Marx hoped to distinguish them from his own brand of 'scientific' socialism. While they were, in his view, naive dreamers and wishful thinkers, lacking the resolve for revolutionary conflict, he, on the other hand, was seeking to uncover the historic-economic basis to class-struggle, the dynamic he believed was the driving force of world history. For just as Feudalism had given way to Capitalism, so too must Capitalism, through the unarguable logic of historical development, give way to the next and final stage, Communism. Here we will arrive at the end of history, and with it the end of class struggle, the end of politics and the birth of a new society of unity and freedom:

> When, in the course of development, class distinctions have disappeared, and all production has been concentrated in the whole nation, the public power will lose its political character. Political power, properly so called, is merely the organized power of one class for oppressing another. If the proletariat during its contest with the bourgeoisie is compelled, by the force of circumstances, to organize itself as a class, if, by means of a revolution, it makes itself the ruling class, and, as such, sweeps away by force the old conditions of production, then it will, along with these conditions, have swept away the conditions for the existence of class antagonisms and of classes generally, and will thereby have abolished its own supremacy as a class.
>
> In place of the old bourgeois society, with its classes and class antagonisms, we shall have an association, in which the free development of each is the condition for the free development of all.[11]

Marx and Engels repeatedly emphasise the distinction between utopian and scientific socialism, keen to avoid any charge that they might be guilty of the offence for which they criticised their predecessors. And yet, the more that Marx and his followers proclaim their freedom from the merest taint of utopianism, the more their ideas appear to approach just such a utopian ideal. The fact remains that while Fourier and Owen were willing to put their hypotheses to the test by establishing experimental communities, Marx was secure in the belief that historical determinism would prove him right in the long run. Who is truly the 'scientific' socialist here, one is forced to ask? Indeed, in maintaining faith in a future that will inexorably lead to the attainment of a perfect society, free from the failings, contradictions and inequalities of the present, Marxism seems to resemble not so much a science as a religion.

In his introduction to the *Manifesto*, AJP Taylor questions Marx's scientific credentials, arguing that the only 'novelty' to distinguish his vision from that of earlier utopian dreamers is his belief that the roots to this utopia lie in the practical present, even if we feel otherwise: 'Dialectical materialism would compel men to live in Utopia whatever the promptings of their hearts.'[12] Elsewhere, Taylor describes Marx as a 'prophet, not a philosopher.'[13] And, if Marx is such a figure, then the *Manifesto* is the sacred text of this new religion, a religion that was, for the majority of the twentieth century at least, a conspicuous success, attracting the support, even if only in name, of regimes governing more than half the world's population. Indeed, paradoxically, for a movement that has been so vociferous in undermining the role of utopian thought, Marxism has proved its greatest adherent. 'The high tide of Utopia' that Marxism represents has since abated in dramatic fashion, and yet it remains a potent symbol of both the allure and the danger that the quest for perfection entails.[14]

Edward Bellamy, *Looking Backward*

One of the most influential utopian novels ever written, *Looking Backward 2000 – 1887* (1888) was, remarkably, the bestselling book of its day, becoming only the second American novel to sell more than a million copies.[15] Furthermore, not only did it inspire a host of imitators and fellow utopians to write their own works, but it propelled its author, Edward Bellamy, to the forefront of the Nationalist Movement his book had inspired.

Born in 1850, the son of a Baptist clergyman and a Calvinist mother, Bellamy rejected a career as a barrister in favour of that of a journalist and would-be author. He was, by all accounts, a shy, even reclusive man whose life was utterly transformed by the celebrity generated by *Looking Backward*. From this point on, until his death in 1898, Bellamy became an energetic spokesperson for Nationalist politics; his critique of capitalism and call for an end to class division struck a chord with millions of the unemployed and disaffected at a time when society appeared to be on the brink of momentous change. Born of a reaction against nineteenth-century individualism and an almost spiritual sense of human solidarity, *Looking Backward* was to become a manifesto of sorts to those who were sympathetic to the egalitarian ethos of socialism but were reluctant to embrace its revolutionary politics.

Opening in *fin de siècle* Boston in 1887, Bellamy's novel sees its hero, the wealthy and aristocratic Julian West, fall into a hypnotic sleep. When he awakes, the year is 2000 and the capitalist society that he left behind has been replaced by a more equitable system. From his host, Dr Leete, West learns that America has undergone a bloodless revolution in which the poverty and inequality that characterised nineteenth-century Boston have been replaced by a centralised society governed by a single business syndicate offering both employment for all and an equal share of the profits. This 'Religion of Solidarity', or Nationalism, as it is known politically, is, strictly speaking, not socialism, but monopoly capitalism, or what Bellamy describes as 'public capitalism'.[16] A system which has evolved quite naturally out of the deficiencies of capitalism, as Dr Leete explains:

Early in the last century the evolution was completed by the final consolidation of the entire capital of the nation. The industry and commerce of the country, ceasing to be conducted by a set of irresponsible corporations and syndicates of private persons at their caprice and for their profit, were intrusted to a single syndicate representing the people, to be conducted in the common interest for the common profit... In a word, the people of the United States concluded to assume the conduct of their own business, just as one hundred odd years before they had assumed the conduct of their own government, organizing now for industrial purposes on precisely the same grounds that they had then organized for political purposes. At last, strangely late in the world's history, the obvious fact was perceived that no business is so essentially the public business as the industry and commerce on which the people's livelihood depends, and to entrust it to private persons to be managed for private profit is a folly similar in kind, though vastly greater in magnitude, to that of surrendering the functions of political government to kings and nobles to be conducted for their personal glorification.[17]

In the absence of war (which has been abolished), working life is now regulated with military precision and every man is expected to do his duty. In Bellamy's vision of the ideal future, this duty involves a surprising amount of menial work, and each man is ranked according to the value of his labour. The rewards for such work, however, are distributed equally, with everyone receiving an equal share of the national profit. 'All men who do their best, do the same,' writes Bellamy, and it would appear, are more than happy to do so.[18]

Alongside these disturbingly regimented working practices, Bellamy introduces some more familiar utopian innovations: money has been abolished, as has any notion of wealth or poverty; sexuality, freed from the distractions of wealth or position, is now dependent upon natural selection; through the eradication of poverty and the role of education, crime has been largely eliminated; technological progress has transformed the quality of life – music is piped into every home via telephone, while housework has been made obsolete. From the distance of the twenty-first century, Bellamy's vision of the year 2000 can fluctuate between the sinister and the bizarre. *Looking Backward* is less successful at delineating a vision of an egalitarian future than in depicting the injustices of the era that West has left behind. In the nightmarish final chapter of Bellamy's book, West dreams that he has returned to the Boston of 1887; and it is here, amid the 'moral repulsiveness' of his own city, that West (and Bellamy) most powerfully articulates his indictment of the capitalist system.[19] For *Looking Backward* incorporates both utopian and dystopian elements, displaying the energetic optimism that was the hallmark of early socialist thought as well as highlighting the dystopian anxieties which were to dominate the coming century.

William Morris, *News from Nowhere*

Written as a direct response to Bellamy's *Looking Backward*, *News from Nowhere* (1890) offers a vision of a socialist future quite unlike that of Bellamy and his utopian predecessors. In contrast to Bellamy's belief in the benefits of technological progress and his emphasis upon the value of organised labour, Morris depicts an altogether more romantic image of a pastoral England freed from the horrors of the industrial age. After reading Bellamy's novel in May 1889, Morris responded to it with disdain, commenting, 'I wouldn't care to live in such a cockney paradise as [Bellamy] imagines.'[20] Morris uses the word 'cockney' here to denote a vulgar materialism, and for a man afflicted by the 'ugliness' of the modern world, Bellamy's world-view would have been totally at odds with his own. Indeed, it was this antipathy to Bellamy's work that stimulated Morris to respond with his own utopia, which began to appear in a serialised form the following year.

Despite, or perhaps because of, his privileged background, William Morris (1834–96) was, from an early age, to react against the injustices of the class system. And yet his antagonism to such a system appears to have been as much aesthetic as political, his greatest objection directed not towards economic inequality but at the machine age, which was, in his eyes, responsible both for despoiling the landscape and for enforcing mechanised and regimented working practices. Morris was to respond by supporting a return to the production of old-style handicrafts, and in 1861 he was to found a highly successful company manufacturing the stained glass, textiles and furnishings which were to make his name. Morris was to embrace socialism in the early 1880s, helping to found the Socialist League in 1884. And yet, despite his claims to have studied socialism 'from a scientific point of view'[21], the socialism that he was to espouse in *News from Nowhere* is idiosyncratic in the extreme and displays little evidence of any faith in science, socialist or otherwise. Indeed, Morris appears less interested in a march towards a socialist future than in a retreat to the Middle Ages: an era understood by Morris to mean an unbroken pageant of haymaking, dancing and embroidery.

In *News from Nowhere*, the narrator, William Guest, goes to sleep in late nineteenth-century London, only to wake to a socialist future bearing a striking resemblance to Morris's idiosyncratic vision of the past. In this utopian future, the sun shines over a clean and sparkling Thames, and he is greeted by a population of invariably happy, polite and well-embroidered Londoners. The origins of this remarkable transformation lie in the revolutionary upheaval of 1952, through which, he is informed, the malign influence of the industrial revolution was finally erased:

> 'The change,' said Hammond, 'which in these matters took place very early in our epoch, was most strangely rapid. People flocked into the country villages, and, so to say, flung themselves upon the freed land like a wild beast upon his prey; and in a very little time the villages of England were more populous than they had been since the fourteenth century, and were still growing fast... The town invaded the country; but the invaders, like the warlike invaders of early days, yielded to the influence of their surroundings, and became country people; and in their turn, as they became more numerous than the townsmen, influenced them also; so that the difference between town and country grew less and less, and it was indeed this world of the country vivified by the thought and briskness of town-bred folk which has produced that happy and leisurely but eager life of which you have had a first taste... The crude ideas of the first half of the twentieth century, when men were still oppressed by the fear of poverty, and did not look enough to the present pleasure of ordinary daily life, spoilt a great deal of what the commercial age had left us of external beauty... But slowly as the recovery came, it *did* come; and the more you see of us, the clearer it will be to you that we are happy. That we live amidst beauty without any fear of becoming effeminate; that we have plenty to do, and on the whole enjoy doing it. What more can we ask of life?'[22]

As Guest travels across London with his companion Dick, continuing up the Thames towards Oxfordshire, he is introduced to a society that has wilfully regressed to a pre-industrial age. London and the other major urban centres have been largely dismantled and have reverted to smaller communities set within woodland and rolling meadows. Money and commerce have been abolished, as have all forms of industrial labour, and the population is now happily employed in an array of more pleasurable activities, from the seemingly ubiquitous haymaking to the production of attractive handicrafts. In effect, the workforce has become one great cottage industry, free from the regulation of government (politics has been abolished, and the Houses of Parliament are now a repository for manure) and conducted on an entirely voluntary basis. For work is no longer the necessary evil that Bellamy describes, but rather a source of creativity and joy. There is no legal code or system of formal education, and decisions concerning marriage and divorce are settled within the family. In short, the utopia that Guest discovers presents a remarkably decentralised, almost anarchic, view of a socialist future, in which government is almost wholly absent and where the individual is left to follow his own path to happiness and self-realisation. As the novel ends, Guest awakes, and unlike in Bellamy's novel, where the hero remains in his future paradise, Guest finds himself once again at home in 'dingy Hammersmith', from where he vows to turn his dream into reality.[23]

While many of the utopias of the nineteenth century attempted to outline a vision of society with a firm basis in reality, eager to witness the practical application of their plans, *News from Nowhere*, on the other hand, appears wholly divorced from any such possibility. For the sunny future that Morris envisages, in which a small and stable population enjoys good health and plentiful resources within a bucolic setting, powered, it would appear, only by handicrafts, seems to dispense entirely with any of those awkward social and economic questions that one might expect a socialist utopia to answer. In this sense, William Guest's dream must remain exactly that, for Morris's pre-industrial utopia is truly a return to the Middle Ages, an Arcadian fantasy of material abundance and wish-fulfilment, that has little in common with the pragmatism of Owen and Marx.

Notes

1 Claude-Henri de Saint-Simon, 'Sketch of a New Political System' (1819), in *Selected Writings on Science, Industry and Social Organisation*, ed. and trans. by Keith Taylor, London: Croom Helm, 1975, p. 202–6 (Author's Note), and qtd. in Claeys and Sargent, p. 206.

2 Carey, p. 187.

3 Goldstein, L, 'Early Feminist Themes in French Utopian Socialism: The St-Simonians and Fourier' in *Journal of the History of Ideas*, (1982) Vol.43, No. 1, p.92.

4 Charles Fourier, *The Utopian Vision of Charles Fourier: Selected Texts on Work, Love and Passionate Attraction*, ed. and trans. by Jonathan Beecher and Richard Bienvenu, London, Jonathan Cape, 1972, and qtd. in Carey, p. 212.

5 Carey, p. 211.

6 Robert Owen, *A New View of Society and Other Writings*, ed. by Gregory Claeys, London: Penguin, 1991, Introduction, p. xxiii.

7 Owen, p. 32.

8 Owen, p. 35.

9 Carey, p. 207.

10 Karl Marx and Friedrich Engels, *The Communist Manifesto* (1848), trans. by Samuel Moore, ed. by AJP Taylor, Harmondsworth: Penguin, 1967, p. 117.

11 Marx, *Communist Manifesto*, p. 105.

12 AJP Taylor, 'Introduction', in Karl Marx and Friedrich Engels, *The Communist Manifesto* (1848), trans. by Samuel Moore, ed. by AJP Taylor, Harmondsworth: Penguin, 1967, p. 10.

13 Taylor, p. 27.

14 Levin, p. 102.

15 Edward Bellamy, *Looking Backward 2000 – 1887*, ed. by Matthew Beaumont, Oxford: Oxford University Press, 2007, Introduction, p. vii. The novel's extraordinary popularity had been outstripped previously only by Harriet Beecher Stowe's *Uncle Tom's Cabin* (1852).

16 Bellamy, *Looking Backward*, Introduction, p. xvii.

17 Bellamy, *Looking Backward*, p. 33.

18 Carey, p. 285.

19 Bellamy, p. 183.

20 William Morris, *News from Nowhere*, ed. by David Leopold, Oxford: Oxford University Press, 2003, Introduction, p. xii.

21 Morris, *News from Nowhere*, Introduction, p. ix.

22 Morris, *News from Nowhere*, p. 61.

23 Morris, *News from Nowhere*, p. 181.

Totalitarian Nightmares

Dominated by the prophetic warnings of Wells and Huxley, Zamyatin and Orwell, the first half of the twentieth century may be seen as predominantly, but not exclusively, dystopian. In the early years of the new century HG Wells continued to outline his vision of a socialist future, the idea which had dominated utopian thought during the previous century. But such dreams of peace and prosperity were soon to give way to darker imaginings, as the brutal realities of twentieth-century history began to unfold. Soon utopian thought was to be characterised not by images of global harmony and cooperation but rather by presentiments of war and oppression, as the ideological horrors of fascism and communism appeared on the horizon. The spectre of totalitarian rule was to fuel the growth of the dystopian genre during the inter-war years, as questions of individual freedom, race and gender were played out in an array of dispiriting scenarios. By 1945, as the true scale of Nazi atrocities was revealed, the ideas that had animated Wells's generation were finally discredited, and the utopian tradition itself appeared to have been curtailed.

HG Wells, *A Modern Utopia*

The first thing to say about *A Modern Utopia* is that it is unique amongst the entries in this chapter in that Wells intended his text to be read as a sincere and positive attempt to outline an ideal society. Unfortunately, however, *A Modern Utopia* is also a perfect example of the ways in which changing intellectual fashions and unforeseen historical events can conspire to undermine and ultimately transform the most well-intentioned utopian visions into dystopian nightmares.

HG Wells is perhaps the best-known and certainly the most prolific of all twentieth-century utopian writers. Almost single-handedly responsible for the emergence of science fiction as a mainstream genre, his 'scientific romances', such as *The Time Machine* (1895), *The Island of Doctor Moreau* (1896), *The War of the Worlds* (1898) and *The First Men in the Moon* (1901), all contain clear utopian, or more commonly dystopian, elements within them, extrapolating from current events and scientific innovations to depict possible futures for mankind. Later works offer more explicit outlines of his hopes and fears for the future: *Men Like Gods* (1923) and *The Shape of Things To Come* (1933) are written in a broadly optimistic vein, underpinned by a faith in the power of science to overcome all obstacles to human progress. While *When the Sleeper Wakes* (1899, revised 1910), *Anticipations* (1901) and *The World Set Free* (1914) emphasise recurrent concerns about overpopulation, social breakdown and environmental catastrophe.

It is in *A Modern Utopia* (1905), however, that Wells offers his most comprehensive outline of a society reflecting his desire for a single World State. The plot, as far as one exists, describes the experiences of two English travellers on a walking holiday in the Swiss Alps who find themselves transported to another world. This other planet is physically identical with our own but is governed according to utopian principles. Through successive chapters the structure of this utopian world is revealed, as questions of economics, personal freedom, sexual and racial equality, political power and social organisation are given detailed consideration. Returning from Switzerland to a utopian London, one of our travellers, who bears an uncanny resemblance to Wells himself, is introduced to his utopian self, before the dream ends abruptly and they both find themselves back in the shabby reality of the Edwardian city.

From the outset, Wells's alternate world appears remarkably pleasant: the population seems invariably healthy, well-educated and content; they are well-dressed and their cities are clean, efficient and attractively designed; war, poverty and the extremes of inequality have been abolished; all share in a common language and culture while maintaining a distinct creative and intellectual identity; there is complete sexual and racial harmony; while this single World-State is governed by a class of benevolent, self-sacrificing and voluntarily appointed rulers called the Samurai. In comparison to this best of all possible worlds, our own is revealed to be hopelessly flawed. And yet, amidst this apparent perfection, the reader is struck by some far less appetising details. For instance, in an ideal world, what is one to do with that section of the population that stubbornly persists in falling short of perfection?

Most Utopias present themselves as going concerns, as happiness in being; they make it an essential condition that a happy land can have no history, and all the citizens one is permitted to see are well looking and upright and mentally and morally in tune... it is our business to ask what Utopia will do with its congenital invalids, its idiots and madmen, its drunkards and men of vicious mind, its cruel and furtive souls, its stupid people, too stupid to be of use to the community, its lumpish, unteachable and unimaginative people?... These people will have to be in the descendent phase, the species must be engaged in eliminating them; there is no escape from that, and conversely the people of exceptional quality must be ascendant. The better sort of people, so far as they can be distinguished, must have the fullest freedom of public service, and the fullest opportunity of parentage. And it must be open to every man to approve himself worthy of ascendency.[1]

In previous utopias such as Plato's *Republic*, upon which Wells models much of his account, there is often an underclass that coexists with its utopian neighbours without sharing in any of their freedoms. But, in the absence of slavery, what is one to do with society's outcasts? For Wells, the solution was eugenics. In Wells's utopia, the 'feeble and spiritless' must be identified, isolated from the community, and once denied the right to reproduce, they must be gradually bred out of the population. Happily oblivious to the Nazi atrocities that lay ahead, Wells, like many of his contemporaries, believed that evolutionary theory and scientific progress held out the possibility of improving the racial qualities of future generations.[2]

If, in the light of twentieth-century history, Wells's belief in eugenics now appears horribly misjudged, his error is compounded by his belief in a ruling class of 'voluntary noblemen'. If the lowest strata of society, or as his utopians put it, the 'base' elements of the population, are to be eliminated, Wells's plans for his ruling class now appear equally unfortunate, dispensing with the inefficiencies of electoral democracy in favour of a benign dictatorship. Wells devotes great detail to 'the Rule', the arduous and almost monastic code of conduct by which his Samurai rulers will live and govern, but the idea of a self-appointed administrative elite holds little appeal for the modern reader. And, as Francis Wheen points out in his introduction to *A Modern Utopia*, Wells's tribute to some of the organisational methods of the Soviet Communist Party and the Italian Fascists goes some way to explaining the relative disdain with which his political writings are now regarded.[3] For, despite the well-intentioned and imaginative solutions that Wells adopts in his depiction of a world free from the privations, inequalities and class-bound stupidities of early twentieth-century society, the central and unavoidable feature of his utopia is one of control. In the World State that Wells envisages, the fingerprints and details of the entire population are catalogued upon one vast international database which can at any given moment reveal the movements of its subjects. In 1905, such an innovation might have appeared to Wells and his readers an eminently sensible means of ensuring an efficiently-run society, but a century later, as our own widespread resistance to Government ID cards illustrates, one era's dreams have become the nightmares of succeeding generations.

Jack London, *The Iron Heel*

A forerunner to the celebrated trilogy of dystopias, *We*, *Brave New World* and *Nineteen Eighty-Four*, and rather neglected by comparison, Jack London's *The Iron Heel* acts as a bridge between the socialist utopias of the late nineteenth century, and the totalitarian visions that were to dominate the first half of the twentieth century. First published in 1908, London's novel describes with prescient detail the emergence of global fascism. Unlike Zamyatin and Orwell, however, London's warning of future oppression is not directed towards a socialist dictatorship, but against the oppression of the poor by the rich, as the forces of capital seek to eliminate the threat of organised labour.

A century on, and London's later works still remain in the shadow of his earlier successes, such as *Son of the Wolf* (1900) and *The Call of the Wild* (1903). But, as early as 1896, the young Jack London (1876-1916) was known as 'the Boy Socialist of Oakland'[4], and concern for the plight of the working-class was to be displayed throughout his work, most notably in an earlier book, *The People of the Abyss* (1903), his account of the poverty he witnessed in London's East End. London's short but picaresque life in which he was employed variously as an oyster pirate, gold prospector and reporter, is at least as well known as his fiction. But despite his reputation as a perpetual outsider and champion of the underdog, it is often forgotten that, by the time of his death, London was possibly the best known, and certainly the best paid, writer in the world, a position that can sit uncomfortably with his role as working-class hero. Indeed, London's own take on social-ism was by no means a straightforward one, his prolific consumption of philosophy and history resulting in a pecu-liar world-view that owed at least as much to Nietzsche as it did to Marx. As a consequence, *The Iron Heel* has appealed to a wide and often unexpected readership. Trotsky was to praise the novel's remarkable 'historical foresight', but London's book has more recently been listed as a recom-mended text on white supremacist websites.[5]

London uses the device of a fictional manuscript to lend credence to his tale, and *The Iron Heel* purports to be based upon the 'Everhard Manuscript', an account of the revolu-tionary struggle of early twentieth-century America, which is subsequently discovered some seven centuries later in around 2600 AD, or 419 BOM as it is now dated, the Brotherhood of Man having finally been attained some 300 years after the events retold here. This futuristic setting is supported by copious footnotes which aim to construct a plausible historical context within which London's account can be read, but otherwise *The Iron Heel* is a straightforward and at times overbearing blend of socialist tract and historical speculation.

The narrator of the manuscript is Avis Everhard, wife to the novel's hero, the socialist revolutionary, lover, and it would seem, Jack London impersonator, Earnest Everhard, to the modern ear, perhaps the most ludicrously named revolutionary in all literature. Spanning the years between 1912 and 1932, the Manuscript describes the gradual emergence and ultimate victory of the Oligarchy, or Iron Heel, in the United States and across the globe, as an alliance of monopoly trusts supported by the military and state combine to crush the middle class and violently suppress the proletariat. Everhard recalls how early political arguments soon give way to more sinister developments. Free speech is curtailed, workers' rights are abolished, and socialist activists are arrested and executed. Soon small businessmen and farmers are bankrupted and their property appropriated as the Iron Heel assumes total control over economic production and political power. The Mercenaries, a vast military organisation, act on behalf of the Iron Heel to ruthlessly hunt down and destroy all socialist sympathisers, forcing Everhard and his supporters underground into small revolutionary cells. The sole purpose of the Iron Heel, and its entire philosophy, is the maintenance of political power at all costs. The rich and the powerful have always dominated the poor and the weak, and as one of the Oligarchs, Mr Wickson, makes plain to Everhard, they always will:

This, then, is our answer. We have no words to waste on you. When you reach out your vaunted strong hands for our palaces and purpled ease, we will show you what strength is. In roar of shell and shrapnel and in whine of machine-guns will our answer be couched. We will grind you revolutionists down under our heel, and we shall walk upon your faces. The world is ours, we are its lords, and ours it shall remain. As for the host of labor, it has been in the dirt since history began, and I read history aright. And in the dirt it shall remain so long as I and mine and those that come after us have the power. There is the word. It is the king of words — Power. Not God, not

Mammon, but Power. Pour it over your tongue till it tingles with it. Power.[6]

The novel concludes with the violent suppression of the first revolt against the Oligarchy, as the proletariat rises up in Chicago, only to be slaughtered in their thousands. But before the dust has settled, Everhard is looking forward to a further revolt against the Iron Heel, unaware that three hundred years of bloodshed will pass before final victory is secured.

Set in the years immediately following those in which it was written, *The Iron Heel* is grounded in the poverty and nascent socialism that characterised America before the First World War. But London's attempts to extrapolate from current events were often wide of the mark: International Socialism is defeated by Nationalism and is unable to prevent World War I; the Middle Class in America is not crushed but rather grows exponentially; Fascism arrives, but in Europe and the Far East. In other respects, however, London's novel is truly prophetic, particularly in his description of the ways in which an unholy alliance of big business, the military and the political elites unite in the face of a threat to their supremacy, deploying the entire state apparatus to isolate, undermine and eliminate the labour movement. Elsewhere, he predicts the growth of the secret police and surveillance culture; the role of political propaganda and control of the media; the suppression of free speech and the subversion of education; the emergence of domestic terrorism and home-grown militias; the formation of urban ghettoes and the marginalisation of an economic underclass.

The Iron Heel demonstrates London's faith in the classical Marxist creed of historical materialism, in which socialism is held to be the inevitable successor to feudalism and capitalism. But despite his socialist credentials and his outspoken opposition to fascism, London's philosophy is less clear-cut than it appears. Indeed, like HG Wells, London's political views have been rather undermined by his support for less palatable ideas that were fashionable in his day but which have been subsequently discredited. Elements of Social Darwinism, for example, an individualistic belief in the survival of the fittest, are expressed throughout London's work, as are theories of racial supremacy that were later to become the hallmark of the fascist movement. It is for this reason, perhaps, that Orwell was to claim that had London lived to see the arrival of the conflict he had predicted, it would be unclear which side he would choose to support. And it is because of these political inconsistencies, as well as the clear deficiencies of his prose style, that London's novel remains overshadowed by later dystopias that were, in many cases, to prove less prophetic than his own.

Yevgeny Zamyatin, *We*

The first, and perhaps the greatest, of the trilogy of major twentieth-century dystopias that also includes Huxley's *Brave New World* and Orwell's *Nineteen Eighty-Four*, Yevgeny Zamyatin's *We* was written in 1920 but was banned in the Soviet Union. It was finally made available to his countrymen in 1988, sixty-four years after it had first been published in English.

Born in Lebedyan in rural Russia in 1884 and dying in

exile in Paris in 1937, Zamyatin spent two years in England during the First World War working in the Tyneside shipyards. A naval architect by profession, Zamyatin returned to Russia on the eve of the October revolution where he was to become a lecturer in literature. A fluent English speaker, Zamyatin was to translate a number of English and American writers, amongst them HG Wells, who was to prove a major influence upon his work. Zamyatin regarded Wells's novels not as utopias but rather as examples of 'socio-fantasy', a new and hybrid literary form expressed through 'social pamphlets disguised as science-fiction novels'.[7] Wells had created the perfect vehicle for offering a critique of the contemporary age while anticipating the era to come, and Zamyatin's *We* may be read as an attempt to form an equivalent account of early twentieth-century Russia. But where Zamyatin was to surpass Wells was in his ability not only to capture the spirit of his own age but to depict so prophetically the political evolution of post-revolutionary Soviet society. Indeed, many readers of Zamyatin's totalitarian vision immediately recognise a satire on Stalinist rule, unaware that *We* actually predates Stalin's rise to power.[8]

We is a nightmarish vision of the ultimate controlled society. In a glass-enclosed city of mathematical precision lives a population of nameless individuals, survivors of a devastating war. The inhabitants of the One State have numbers rather than names and follow a carefully monitored routine. Their glass environment allows them to be watched at all times; conversations are recorded; sexual relations are governed by the state; food is chemically derived from naphtha; natural life has been eradicated. In such a society, the inhabitants can no longer contemplate a life lived freely and without state intervention:

> I will be quite frank: even we do not have an absolute, exact solution to the problem of happiness: twice a day (from 16.00 to 17.00 and from 21.00 to 22.00) our mighty unipersonal organism disintegrates into separate cells; these are the Personal Hours, as fixed by The Tables of Hourly Commandments... Yet I firmly believe (let them call me an idealist and phantaseur!) – I believe that sooner or later the day will come when we shall find a place in the general formula for these hours also, a day when all of its 86,400 seconds will be included in The Tables of Hourly Commandments.
>
> I have had occasion to read and hear many incredible things concerning those times when people were still living in a free – i.e. an unorganized, savage – state. But the one thing that has always struck me as the most improbable was precisely this: How could the governing power (let us say even a rudimentary one) allow the people to live without anything resembling our Table of Hourly Commandments, without obligatory walks, without exact regulation of mealtimes – how could it allow them to get up and go to bed whenever they got the notion to do so?[9]

Any deviation from the proscribed regulations is met with the harshest of punishments. Infringements are reported to the Operational Division and suspects are interrogated and then asphyxiated under the Gas Bell Glass. Executions are carried out personally by the ruler of the One State, the Benefactor, and are administered by the Machine, a device which reduces the body to 'a puddle of chemically pure water'.[10] And yet, in the midst of this perfectly ordered world of unfeeling rationality, the mathematician, D-503 falls in love with the woman, E-330. E-330 is a member of an underground movement, Mephis, which plans to destroy the Glass Wall which surrounds the One State, returning its inhabitants to the natural world. Before these plans can be carried out, the state is saved by its scientists, who discover a surgical means for eradicating the human imagination. The Fantasiectomy is to be applied to all inhabitants, and despite an attempt to escape, D-503 is also subjected to this procedure. Soon he has been freed from what he now regards as his former sickness, and is able to betray E-330 and her organisation to the Guardians, government spies, without experiencing any guilt or unwanted emotional response. As the novel closes, he watches calmly alongside the Benefactor as E-330 and her fellow conspirators are tortured beneath the Gas Bell before facing execution. The betrayal of rationality has been defeated.

Denied an audience in Zamyatin's homeland, *We* has proven enormously influential elsewhere, especially in the Anglophone world where it has acted as a bridge between the late nineteenth-century dystopian fictions of HG Wells and the generation of writers that followed.[11] In particular, the works of Huxley and Orwell outlined later owe their inspiration to Zamyatin, who was to illustrate with frightening clarity the consequences of a marriage between scientific progress and political ideology.

Aldous Huxley, *Brave New World*

Like HG Wells's *A Modern Utopia*, to which *Brave New World* is a satirical response, Huxley's utopia also depicts a single World State in which the masses coexist in apparent harmony. Scientific advances have eliminated disease and hunger and a contented population live pleasurable lives free from pain and want. But Huxley did not share Wells's optimistic sense of the future, and he remained sceptical of the benefits of a single socialist state exerting benevolent control over its citizens. Instead, he foresaw a future in which individual identity would be threatened by the homogenising effects of mass consumption, a future that was grounded in the Americanisation of European culture. *Brave New World* was written in 1931 while Huxley was living in France, but the imaginative impetus for the book was provided by his experiences of America, which he had first visited in the 1920s. Huxley regarded American values as being essentially opposed to what we might call High Culture, instead promoting a bland uniformity underpinned by commercially induced dreams of material satisfaction. It is out of these fears of a mass-produced future that *Brave New World* was born.

With clear echoes of Zamyatin's *We*, a novel which Huxley claimed not to have been aware of at the time, *Brave New World* is situated in a post-apocalyptic future in which society is rigidly controlled. Set in London in 2540 AD, or 632 AF, according to the new calendar, in which the God of mass-production, Henry Ford, has come to replace Christ, Huxley extrapolates from the admiration of his contemporaries for eugenics to depict a future of state-controlled reproduction. Natural childbirth is now obsolete; instead children are artificially produced and delivered in Hatcheries and Conditioning Centres. By varying the supply of oxygen to the embryos, intelligence and physical growth can be arrested, resulting in the creation of five individual castes, from the Alphas, who are allowed to develop naturally and are born to form the elite of society, to the Betas, Gammas, Deltas, and finally, the semi-moronic Epsilons to whom the menial tasks are allocated. To ensure that each individual is perfectly adjusted to his artificially assigned station in life, these eugenic interventions are supplemented by the process of 'hypnopaedia', in which recorded voices are repeated during sleep, reinforcing a message of rigid class distinction:

At the end of the room a loud-speaker projected from the wall. The Director walked up to it and pressed a switch.

'...all wear green,' said a soft but very distinct voice, beginning in the middle of a sentence, 'and Delta children wear khaki. Oh no, I don't want to play with Delta children. And Epsilons are still worse. They're too stupid to be able to read or write. Besides, they wear black, which is such a beastly colour. I'm *so* glad I'm a Beta.'

There was a pause; then the voice began again.

'Alpha children wear grey. They work much harder than we do, because they're so frightfully clever. I'm really awfully glad I'm a Beta, because I don't work so hard. And then we are much better than the Gammas and Deltas. Gammas are stupid. They all wear green, and Delta children wear khaki. Oh no, I *don't* want to play with Delta children. And Epsilons are still worse. They're too stupid to be able...'

The Director pushed back the switch. The voice was silent. Only its thin ghost continued to mutter from beneath the eighty pillows.[12]

With people happily conditioned to perform their allotted tasks, any residual discontentment is eradicated through the officially encouraged consumption of 'soma', a hallucinogenic drug which allows the user an enjoyable and guilt-free escape from one's otherwise perfect existence. Further distractions are provided by 'feelies', films in which all the senses are stimulated by electrodes in the seats. Stimulation is also provided in the form of recreational sexual activity which, in the absence of family ties and natural reproduction, is simply regarded as another form of social interaction.

Huxley's novel follows two characters, Lenina, a Beta-Minus, and Bernard, an Alpha-Plus, as they come to question their society and their pre-ordained positions within it. On a trip to a Savage Reservation in New Mexico, Bernard and Lenina discover a world beyond the comfortable conformity of their own. Attracted to the unfamiliar behaviour of the natives, Bernard decides to return to London with a pet savage, John. At first welcomed by his new society, John soon turns against it, disgusted by its shallow pursuit of pleasure. Isolating himself from society in a lighthouse outside London, John soon becomes a tourist attraction, and unable to escape the crowds of sightseers intrigued by his 'uncivilised' behaviour, he hangs himself.

Huxley was to return to the themes set out in *Brave New World* some thirty years later in his non-fiction work *Brave New World Revisited* (1958). In the original novel, Huxley projected his dystopia some six hundred years into the future, but on returning to assess his account in light of the horrors the world had witnessed in the intervening period, Huxley was to revise that estimate, now arguing that *Brave New World* could become a reality in less than a century.[13] Despite the antipathy Huxley had earlier demonstrated towards American culture in *Brave New World*, he was to spend his final years living in California and it was here that he was to write his final work, *Island* (1962). In this book, Huxley portrays a tropical island, Pala, whose inhabitants have discovered the twin joys of Buddhism and LSD. Free love is also encouraged, and it is easy to see why Huxley was later to find an enthusiastic new audience in the counter-cultural movement of the 1960s.

An unlikely prophct for New Age ideas, Huxley's final work demonstrates a more ambivalent, if not supportive, attitude towards many of the elements of his earlier dystopia: sexual promiscuity is now shameless not shameful; drug-taking has become mind expanding rather than mind-numbing; and eugenic practices are now viewed as a necessary means of eradicating genetic imperfections. The young man's dystopia has become, in many respects, the older man's utopia. But where Huxley remains constant is in his resistance to consumerism and mass-consumption. It is his recognition of the power that the mass-market wields in shaping individual thought that still resonates most powerfully today and which ensures *Brave New World* its lasting relevance. Indeed, of the great twentieth-century dystopias, it is Huxley's that most keenly anticipates the more pernicious characteristics of twenty-first century society.

Katherine Burdekin, *Swastika Night*

Published in 1937 under the pseudonym 'Murray Constantine', and re-issued in 1940, Katherine Burdekin's *Swastika Night* is one of several anti-fascist dystopias to appear in the late 1930s and 1940s, and describes an alternate future in which the Nazis have triumphed. Setting aside Hitler's own contribution to the utopian genre in *Mein Kampf* (1924), a work which has been described as terminating such a tradition[14], *Swastika Night* is the earliest attempt to depict, in fictional form, the consequences of such a victory, particularly in its focus on the impact on women.

Burdekin sets her novel seven hundred years into the future, as the Nazi Thousand Year Reich continues its subjugation of both women and the lesser races. In this neo-feudal nightmare, power is divided between Germany and Japan who coexist in a state of permanent, if unacknowledged, peace. The Jews have been exterminated, Christianity survives in a debased and despised form, and England, along with Europe and much of the Western World, worships Adolf Hitler as a God. Women have been totally subjugated to men, and are regarded as little more than cattle, breeders whose role is to continue the race, and who have been deprived of all rights. History has been erased, books destroyed and language has been distorted to provide retrospective support for this worldview, a philosophy which is inculcated through the catechism of Nazi doctrine:

As a woman is above a worm,
So is a man above a woman.
As a woman is above a worm,
So is a worm above a Christian...
So, my comrades, the lowest thing,
The meanest, filthiest thing
That crawls on the face of the earth
Is a Christian woman.
To touch her is the uttermost defilement
For a German man.
To speak to her only is a shame.
They are all outcast, the man, the woman and the child.
My sons, forget it not!
On pain of death or torture
Or being cut off from the blood. Heil Hitler.[15]

In this Nazi future, human relationships have been reduced to a blend of acutely felt misogyny and an unspoken homo-eroticism, concealed beneath the martial virtues of strength and violence. Denied a history, or even the posses-sion of a soul, women have become so degraded that their own self-loathing has begun to have unforeseen conse-quences. Adapting biologically to a hostile environment, they are no longer producing enough daughters to ensure the survival of the race. Nazi society has begun to stagnate, and amidst this world of blind conformity and thuggish brutality, some are beginning to question the philosophy under which they live.

One such individual, an Englishman named Alfred (surnames have been banned), visits his old friend Hermann in Germany, where he is introduced to an old

Nazi aristocrat in possession of the truth about Hitler and the evolution of German society. Alfred is entrusted with a book that outlines the pre-Nazi past in which Hitler is revealed in his human form, and in which the current status of women is challenged. Vowing to protect this secret until the time comes at which Nazi society will be overthrown, Alfred and Hermann return to England, concealing the book at Stonehenge. The novel concludes with their deaths at the hands of the Nazis, but the book is passed on to Alfred's son for safekeeping.

Like the secret text that Burdekin's novel describes, *Swastika Night* itself disappeared from view after the war, only to be rediscovered in 1985 by an American academic who confirmed Burdekin as the author and encouraged its re-publication. With its hostility to male-dominated society, *Swastika Night* is now read as a classic feminist dystopia and yet, as Daphne Patai has indicated, the reality of Nazi ideology was somewhat different. For the health and welfare of racially desirable women were, in fact, promoted by Nazi policy, and motherhood was supported through a series of laws providing maternity benefits and marriage incentives for those able to produce 'hereditarily valuable' offspring for the nation.[16] Burdekin's crucial insight lay in her recognition of the ideological link between the apotheosis of motherhood, and the reduction of women to the role of mere breeders.[17] Furthermore, in its pioneering identification of fascism as a logical extension of patriarchal society, *Swastika Night* prefigures much contemporary feminist theory. Indeed, in its depiction of a future that has erased its past, and in which language has been appropriated by the state, *Swastika Night* also anticipates Orwell's *Nineteen Eighty-Four*, which was to be published twelve years later. There is no evidence to suggest that Orwell had read *Swastika Night* before 1949, but as we shall see, the two novels have a great deal in common, not least in their accounts of the ways in which human relationships are distorted by totalitarian regimes.

George Orwell, *Nineteen Eighty-Four*

The most famous of all dystopias and one of the very greatest novels of the twentieth century, *Nineteen Eighty-Four* (Orwell insisted that the title should be written out in full) was published in 1949 and provides the definitive fictional account of totalitarian oppression. From Big Brother to Room 101, Newspeak to the Thought Police, Orwell's novel has also had a major impact on the English language, his ideas becoming bywords for surveillance culture and governmental control.

Orwell's literary influences include both Jack London's *The Iron Heel* and Huxley's *Brave New World*, as well as Zamyatin's *We* and HG Wells's *A Modern Utopia*. But the major models for *Nineteen Eight-Four* are drawn from Orwell's own experiences. According to his biographer, Michael Shelden, this influence is three-fold: his childhood memories of being bullied at St Cyprian's prep school; witnessing violence as a member of the Burmese Police; and his wartime experiences in the BBC's propaganda department. All were to provide ample evidence of human cruelty and suffering, helping to establish the rather bleak view of human nature that informs his work.[18]

Set in Oceania, a totalitarian super-state in a perpetual

state of war with its neighbours, Eurasia and Eastasia, *Nineteen Eighty-Four* takes place in London, now the major city of the province Airstrip One. Here, the novel's chief protagonist, Winston Smith, is employed at the Ministry of Truth where his job is to falsify historical documents so that they provide retrospective validation for the Party. In a similar structure to Zamyatin's *We*, the events of *Nineteen Eighty-Four* follow Winston Smith on his journey from faithful state employee, through his illicit love affair with co-worker Julia and his intellectual awakening, and on to his final capture, imprisonment and re-education.

Living in a squalid one-room flat and subsisting on a diet of black bread, synthetic meals and gin, Winston's every move is monitored via the two-way television screens that dominate every private and public space. 'Big Brother is Watching You!' proclaim the ubiquitous posters of the Party's leader, and any form of deviant or erratic thought or action results in torture and execution at the hands of the Thought Police. This grimly oppressive existence is broken by the arrival of Julia, a mechanic, with whom he begins a clandestine affair. Together they rent a room in the city's proletarian neighbourhood, where, or so they believe, they can enjoy some privacy beyond the all-seeing eyes of the Party. But there can be no such sanctuary in Orwell's nightmarish vision, for Winston and Julia have been betrayed to the Thought Police. What follows is Winston's interrogation at the Ministry of Love. Here, in dialogue with Party member, O'Brien, Winston is informed that prior to his execution he will be re-educated to accept unquestioningly the Party view. To this end he is subjected to electroshock torture before finally being taken to Room 101, the most feared room in the Ministry. It is here that his re-education will be completed as he is forced to face his greatest fear:

'The worst thing in the world,' said O'Brien, 'varies from individual to individual. It may be burial alive, or death by fire, or by drowning, or by impalement, or fifty other deaths. There are cases where it is some quite trivial thing, not even fatal.'

He had moved a little to one side, so that Winston had a better view of the thing on the table. It was an oblong wire cage with a handle on the top for carry-ing it by. Fixed to the front of it was something that looked like a fencing mask, with the concave side outwards. Although it was three or four metres away from him, he could see that the cage was divided lengthways into two compartments, and that there was some kind of creature in each. They were rats.

'In your case,' said O'Brien, 'the worst thing in the world happens to be rats.'

A sort of premonitory tremor, a fear of he was not certain what, had passed through Winston as soon as he caught his first glimpse of the cage. But at this moment the meaning of the mask-like attachment in front of it suddenly sank into him. His bowels seemed to turn to water.

'You can't do that!' he cried out in a high cracked voice. 'You couldn't, you couldn't! It's impossible.'[19]

Broken by this experience and having wilfully betrayed Julia rather than endure the unendurable, Winston is released pending his execution. He encounters Julia in a park only to find that they have been cured of their feelings for one another. For as the novel closes, Winston realises that he has finally come to love Big Brother.

Often regarded as an attack upon socialism, Orwell was to refute this suggestion publicly, claiming that *Nineteen Eighty-Four* was targeted instead at all forms of totalitarian oppression, both Communist and Fascist. Big Brother is clearly based upon the figure of Josef Stalin and many elements of the novel are based upon the practices of Soviet Communism. But the everyday representations of grinding poverty, set against a backdrop of newspaper-generated imperialist fervour, have their roots in the post-war austerity and imperial decline of Britain in 1948.

Of course, 1984 has come and gone without Britain experiencing the oppression that Orwell's novel antici-pates, and simply as a piece of historical speculation, *Nineteen Eighty-Four* has proved less successful than many of its dystopian counterparts. Such is the moral integrity of Orwell's work, however, allied to his genius as a writer, that *Nineteen Eighty-Four* succeeds in transcending all speci-ficities of time and place, taking its place at the pinnacle of the dystopian tradition. Endlessly replicated but never surpassed, *Nineteen Eighty-Four* remains as relevant today as ever before, continuing to act as a reminder of the ease with which political ideology can distort history and language in support of its own agenda.

Notes

[1] HG Wells, *A Modern Utopia*, ed. by Gregory Claeys and

Patrick Parrinder, London: Penguin, 2005, p. 95.

2 Wells, *A Modern Utopia*, Introduction, p. xviii.

3 Wells, *A Modern Utopia*, Introduction, p. xxiv.

4 Jack London, *The Iron Heel*, ed. by Jonathan Auerbach, London: Penguin, 2006, Introduction, p. viii.

5 London, *The Iron Heel*, Introduction, p. vii.

6 London, *The Iron Heel*, p. 73.

7 Yevgeny Zamyatin, *We*, ed. by Michael Glenny, trans. by Bernard Guilbert Guerney, Harmondsworth: Penguin, 1972, Introduction, p. 11.

8 Carey, p. 387.

9 Zamyatin, p. 29.

10 Carey, p. 387.

11 Zamyatin, Introduction, p. 18.

12 Aldous Huxley, *Brave New World*, London: Grafton, 1977, p. 41.

13 Huxley, *Brave New World*, Foreword (1946), p. 16.

14 Carey, p. 423.

15 Katharine Burdekin (Murray Constantine), *Swastika Night*, ed. by Daphne Patai, New York: The Feminist Press, 1985, p. 7.

16 Katherine Burdekin, *Swastika Night*, Introduction, p. xi. Daphne Patai identifies Otto Weininger's *Sex and Character* (1903) as the likely source for Burdekin's description of Nazi attitudes towards women.

17 Patai, Introduction, p. xi.

18 Michael Shelden, *Orwell: The Authorised Biography*, London: Heinemann, 1991, pp 430–434.

19 George Orwell, *Nineteen Eighty-Four*, ed. by Peter Davison, London: Penguin, 1989, p. 296.

The Cold War to the Present

The Allied victory in the Second World War did little to dispel the sense of foreboding that had characterised the utopian genre in the pre-war years. The advent of the Cold War and the Nuclear Age were to provide freshly apocalyptic scenarios for dystopian futures, inaugurating a whole new sub-genre of the 'catastrophe novel'. Soon John Wyndham, JG Ballard and others were producing ever more inventive outlines of a post-apocalyptic planet, as fears of nuclear Armageddon gave way to those of environmental collapse. While such novels remained largely the preserve of the British, American writers were more interested in exploring the consequences of the post-war boom in technology and consumerism. And while much contemporary American science-fiction looked optimistically to a future of gadget-enhanced leisure, novels such as Kurt Vonnegut's *Player Piano* (1952) and Ray Bradbury's *Fahrenheit 451* (1953) were to question the apparent benefits of such technological progress.

By the late 1960s, however, a new mood of optimism began to pervade the utopian genre, as cultural and political shifts towards racial equality, sexual liberation and greater environmental awareness were reflected in more positive visions of the future. Writers such as Ursula K. Le Guin, Marge Piercy, Joanna Russ and Samuel R. Delany were responsible for overturning the dystopian monopoly for the first time in more than half a century. Their success was to be short-lived, however, and by the late 1970s, as the dreams of this era began to fade, so this brief revival of utopian expression began to falter. In subsequent decades, writers such as Margaret Atwood, William Gibson, Octavia Butler and once again, JG Ballard, have simply re-emphasised the predominant position of dystopian narrative, a situation which has led many commentators to question the continued relevance of utopian thought.

Kurt Vonnegut, *Player Piano*

First published in 1952 and re-issued in 1954 under the name *Utopia 14*, *Player Piano* was Vonnegut's first novel. Now regarded as a dystopian classic, *Player Piano* prefigures many of the themes that were to become hallmarks of later works such as *Cat's Cradle* (1963) and *Slaughterhouse Five* (1969), in particular his pessimistic view of human nature and his scepticism towards the avowed benefits of technological progress. Using the player piano, one of the earliest applications of automotive technology, as a metaphor for the novel's description of a society dominated by machines, Vonnegut demonstrates the ways in which our search for a techno-utopia can have some very damaging consequences for mankind. In this respect, Vonnegut follows the lead of earlier dystopian visionaries who have also questioned the prevailing view of technology as a panacea for social ills. Indeed, he openly acknowledges his debt to Aldous Huxley, having 'cheerfully ripped off the plot of *Brave New World*' in the composition of *Player Piano*.[1] In addition, Vonnegut's novel also reflects his own experiences, most notably his employment at General Electric following World War II, where he was to witness first-hand the emergence of computerised technology and the consequent obsolescence of skilled labour. His resignation from the firm to become a full-time writer, and the effects of this decision upon his relationship with his father, are also clearly replayed within the novel.

Set in Illium, New York, in the aftermath of the Third World War, *Player Piano* depicts a rigidly structured society controlled by a ruling class of engineers and managers and the machines they have created. This group of highly educated professionals presides over an ever increasing population of redundant workers, their obsolete skills or inadequate intellects rendering them effectively unemployable, fit for nothing except the Army or the despised Reclamation and Reconstruction Corps, the 'Reeks and Wrecks', who undertake only the most menial tasks.

One of the best and brightest of the technocratic elite is Dr Paul Proteus, manager of the Illium industrial plant and son of the late Dr George Proteus, a founding father of this new world order. On the surface, Proteus appears to have it all – respect, wealth, prestige, an attractive wife and a secure future – and yet he finds himself increasingly at odds with his environment as he comes to question the aims of his organisation and the society he is helping to uphold. As he comes into contact with disaffected workers and the socially excluded, so these doubts multiply and eventually he finds himself part of an underground revolutionary movement dedicated to the destruction of the machines. Taking their name from an earlier group of the marginalised and oppressed, the Native Americans, the members of the

Ghost Shirt Society appoint Proteus as their leader, setting
out their beliefs in an open letter to society:

> Men, by their nature, seemingly, cannot be happy
> unless engaged in enterprises that make them feel
> useful. They must, therefore, be returned to partici-
> pation in such enterprises.
>
> I hold, and the members of the Ghost Shirt Society
> hold:
>
> That there must be virtue in imperfection, for Man
> is imperfect, and Man is a creation of God.
>
> That there must be virtue in frailty, for Man is frail,
> and Man is a creation of God.
>
> That there must be virtue in inefficiency, for Man
> is inefficient, and Man is a creation of God.
>
> That there must be virtue in brilliance followed by
> stupidity, for Man is alternately brilliant and stupid,
> and Man is a creation of God.
>
> You perhaps disagree with the antique and vain
> notion of Man's being a creation of God.
>
> But I find it a far more defensible belief than the
> one implicit in intemperate faith in lawless techno-
> logical progress – namely, that man is on earth to
> create more durable and efficient images of himself,
> and hence, to eliminate any justification at all for his
> own continued existence.[2]

Rising up to reclaim America for the working man, the
Ghost Shirt Rebellion proves an unmitigated disaster.
Finally freed from all constraint, and giving full vent to
their accumulated frustrations, this bizarre collection of

discontents and would-be revolutionaries embark upon an orgy of destruction that succeeds in wiping out most of Illium's mechanised infrastructure. Having come this far, however, the revolution runs out of steam, its members no clearer as to their ultimate purpose and unable to agree upon a course of action. As the novel closes, it is the morning after the revolution, and with Illium now a waste-land, Proteus and his fellow leaders tamely hand them-selves in to the authorities.

Beyond its obvious critique of mechanisation, *Player Piano* may be read as a broader assault upon the corpor-atism of modern America. Many aspects of the novel could be viewed as utopian in intention – the unskilled and unemployed are generously supported by the state in terms of housing, healthcare and education; labour saving devices adorn every home; advancement in this society is rigorously meritocratic. And yet, despite all these material gains, something essential has been lost. Centralisation of governmental and economic power has resulted in savings in efficiency and an increased standard of living, but life for the average individual has been divorced from the meaning and purpose which makes it worth living. As a conse-quence, the underclass in Vonnegut's novel displays many of the forms of behaviour that have come to plague modern Western economies: disillusionment and discon-tent amongst the young, alcoholism, drug abuse and casual violence, family breakdown, rising crime and rates of suicide.[3] And in the face of such seemingly intractable problems, allied to an acknowledgement that human history cannot be reversed, the prognosis that Vonnegut offers for mankind is grim. *Player Piano* introduces the reader to the brand of pessimistic fatalism which Vonnegut was to display throughout his career; an outlook that was to become the characteristic expression of the utopian tradition in the post-war era.

Derek Raymond, *A State of Denmark*

Born in 1931, Robin Cook was to write six novels between 1962 and 1971, beginning with a fictional account of his experiences of London low-life, *The Crust on its Uppers*. It was after his return from a lengthy sojourn in France, however, that Cook was to produce, under the name of Derek Raymond, the series of neo-noir novels on which his reputation now rests. Raymond died in 1994, and today novels such as *He Died with his Eyes Open* (1984) and the truly gruesome *I Was Dora Suarez* (1990) completely overshadow his earlier works, amongst them the dystopian curiosity, *A State of Denmark* (1970).

If Orwell's *1984* depicts a London mired in the grim austerity of the post-war years, then *A State of Denmark*, in many ways a late addition to the Orwellian tradition, updates this vision to reflect the economic stagnation of the 1970s. Subtitled, 'A Warning to the Incurious', and bearing the dedication, 'For all victims', this dystopian outline of a fascist England was written by Raymond as a wake-up call to those who believed that England was immune to the totalitarianism that had been so prevalent in Europe. Contrasting an England of brutal repression with a romantic vision of rural Italy, *A State of Denmark* shares Orwell's pessimistic vision in its demonstration of the ease with which democratic values can be subverted.

First published in 1970, and largely overlooked ever since, *A State of Denmark* follows its chief protagonist, the journalist, Richard Watt, from exile in Italy to his enforced deportation to England. Structured in two parts, the opening section is set in the remote Tuscan village of Roccamarittima, where Watt and his wife Magda eke out a precarious existence cultivating their vineyard. Here, amidst the splendour of the Italian countryside, Watt gradually learns the true extent of England's downfall under the Dictator, Jobling. And soon the tranquillity of his existence is threatened as he learns that Jobling, determined to silence any dissenting voices, is negotiating with the Italians to have all English citizens forcibly repatriated. Eventually, an emissary is despatched from the UK to appropriate his property, and shortly afterwards Watt and his wife are deported.

The second part of the book exchanges rural simplicity and endless sunshine for a bleak portrayal of a country now characterised by casual violence, corruption and despair:

Not surprisingly, there isn't the violence you used to see around the streets; no one's got the energy or even the motive, really. All the violence is official these days. Not a mod, rocker or a skinhead to be seen anywhere, not the whisper of a pop song, and you couldn't buy a joint of hash if you were to offer a million quid for it. Nothing on the radio except endless hortatory speeches from Jobling and his henchmen. London is getting dark and getting dirty. There's very little street-lighting at night, because of the curfew, and what there is winks and flutters and doesn't work properly. Nor does the Underground; up to three trains a day get stuck in tunnels; I wouldn't use it for anything... During the day there are a lot more mad people about, of course. I used to love the parks but now I can't bear to go in them; nearly every bench is filled with people staring down between their knees or raving about lost fortunes or best friends who have disappeared, or they wander about between the unkempt trees tearing their clothes, or just lie passively in the long grass, their faces drawn with hunger, staring up at the sky, which I suppose is about the only thing that hasn't changed.[4]

Like Anthony Burgess's *1985*, which draws upon memories of the industrial unrest of the 1970s to depict a dystopian Britain under Trade Union control, *A State of Denmark* also identifies the Labour left as the source from which an authoritarian government emerges. In the face of an apathetic electorate, Jobling and his party, The New Pace, encounter little resistance in their rise to power. Soon Parliament has been disbanded, the unions have been destroyed and those branded racially impure have been deported. Scotland and Wales declare independence, leaving England broken and isolated, as Jobling embarks on a purge of all critics of his regime. A former political journalist, blacklisted by the New Pace, Watt falls into this category, and on his return to England he finds himself incarcerated in a prison camp. Here, his resistance to the state is gradually eroded and, as the novel ends, he is executed by lethal injection.

The true target of Raymond's dystopia is not political ideology but complacency. For, while Watt's Italian neighbours are wary of all engagement with the state, having experienced the reality of fascism under Mussolini, the English lack all such political awareness, steadfast in their belief in the permanence of democracy. Even Watt himself, alert to the dangers that Jobling and his party represent, is unable to act decisively to save himself and his family, despite ample opportunity to do so. In this respect, *A State of Denmark* displays the same underlying fatalism that pervades *1984*, as Richard Watt, like Winston Smith before him, sleepwalks towards his inevitable fate, unable to extricate himself from the nightmarish consequences of his actions.

Ursula K. Le Guin, *The Dispossessed*

Returning to the fictional universe which she had visited in several earlier novels, such as *The Left Hand of Darkness* (1969), Ursula K. Le Guin's *The Dispossessed* (1974) uses the twin planets of Anarres and Urras as the setting for one of the most accomplished utopian novels of the post-war period. Using the traditional utopian device of the imaginary voyage, *The Dispossessed* follows its main protagonist, the brilliant physicist Shevek, on his journey from Anarres to Urras and his eventual return home. Employing a narrative structure that favours the non-linear over the sequential, the reader is repeatedly transported between these two worlds as Le Guin offers a comparison of societies that in many respects resemble our own.

Anarres is a largely barren and inhospitable planet and was populated by settlers from Urras some two centuries earlier. These settlers were revolutionary anarchists who were given the right to live on Anarres and to establish a community free from interference. Here they have subsequently established an anarchist society without government control or any form of authoritarian institution. 200 years later the revolution is beginning to stagnate, as a state of permanent revolution and perpetual change is threatened by the emergence of vested interests and the coercive power of public opinion. Seeking to challenge their seclusion and to spread a message of cooperation between societies, Shevek decides to leave Anarres, accepting an invitation to visit Urras.

But if Anarres is an 'ambiguous utopia', a sincere but flawed attempt to establish an ideal society, free from inequality and war, then Urras is a planet whose society and inhabitants are more like our own. Blessed with an abundance of natural resources which have been largely squandered through greed and waste, Urras is an unmistakeably dystopian world in which the patriarchal capitalism of A-Io is at odds with the authoritarian centralism of Thu. In an allusion to the Cold War animosity between the United States and the Soviet Union, Urras is a planet divided by ideological conflict and war, in which the politically naive Shevek finds himself hopelessly out of his depth. Unable to comprehend a world in which human nature is centred upon aggressive competition rather than mutual cooperation, Shevek is unable to recognise the danger of his position as an emissary from a society whose very existence challenges the political order to which he now finds himself accountable. Gradually Shevek awakens to the reality of his situation, realising that his value to his hosts lies only in his ability to provide them with the scientific theories he possesses. Unwilling to accept the notion of himself or his ideas being treated as the property of the state, he allies himself with an underground group which hopes to establish an egalitarian community modelled on Anarres. As the novel ends, however, the revolutionary uprising his presence has inspired is brutally suppressed. Seeking refuge in an alien embassy, Shevek reveals his scientific secrets, which are to be shared openly between planets, in return for his safe passage back to Anarres.

Meanwhile, in the alternate chapters that are set on Anarres, we learn of the background to the events that led Shevek to decide upon his journey to Urras. Amidst the hardships of eking out an existence on Anarres, the very principles upon which their society rests are being eroded. And as his work comes to challenge the scientific orthodoxies of his community, so Shevek finds himself and his family increasingly ostracised. For as he attempts, unsuccessfully, to remind his fellow inhabitants, unless one is able continuously to question and challenge the principles of one's own society, however free that society regards itself as being, then change will inevitably ossify and renewal will give way to intolerance:

'You see,' he said, 'what we're after is to remind ourselves that we didn't come to Anarres for safety, but for freedom. If we must all agree, all work together, we're no better than a machine. If an individual can't work in solidarity with his fellows, it's his duty to work alone. His duty and his right. We have been denying people that right. We've been saying, more and more often, you must work with the others, you must accept the rule of the majority. But any rule is tyranny. The duty of the individual is to accept *no* rule, to be the initiator of his own acts, to be responsible. Only if he does so will the society live, and change, and adapt, and survive. We are not subjects of a State founded upon law, but members of a society formed upon revolution. Revolution is our obligation: our hope of evolution. "The Revolution is in the individual spirit, or it is nowhere. It is for all, or it is nothing. If it is seen as having any end, it will never truly begin." We can't stop here. We must go on. We must take the risks.'[5]

The Dispossessed is a novel that attempts to remedy the criticism that has traditionally attached itself to the utopian genre, namely the idea that in seeking perfection, utopian societies must be both static, having attained the pinnacle of social evolution, and, of course, unattainable, being at odds with the clear imperfections of human nature. Le Guin acknowledges these problems through a recognition that the suffering and hardships encountered by her utopians are not only necessary but desirable, acting as a cohesive force in maintaining a spirit of mutual reliance. Her ambiguous depiction of anarchist society freely recognises the fallibility of human nature and an inherent urge towards individualism and dominance, arguing that only a society that promotes self-criticism and an encouragement toward perpetual reinvention will be able to prosper and to resist the centralising forces that result from stagnation.

Of course, the values of voluntary cooperation, mutual

tolerance and localised self-sufficiency that form the basis of society on Anarres were also to find recognition in particular forms of human society in the early 1970s. For, like other examples of utopian fiction from this period, such as Samuel Delany's *Triton* (1976), Ernest Callenbach's *Ecotopia* (1975), and as we shall see, Marge Piercy's *Woman on the Edge of Time* (1976), the further into speculative future worlds we travel, the closer we seem to find ourselves to the counter-cultural communities of 1960s and 1970s America. In this respect, Anarres can often feel more like a rather drought-ridden hippie commune in California than a different universe, and at times *The Dispossessed* reads less as science-fiction and more as a political or sociological tract.

Ultimately, the settlers of Anarres are truly the *dispossessed*: both through their own choice in rejecting property and through the scarcity of natural resources provided by their new home. And it is exactly this awareness of the limitations of such an environment and the constraints which they inevitably impose that lends Le Guin's account its clarity. By rejecting the idea of utopia as a society of material abundance, Le Guin pares down her vision to reveal the very real possibility of equality and personal fulfilment within the context of hardship and suffering. Indeed, the central message of the book appears to be that one cannot attain the one without an acceptance of the other. And while, like all utopias, Le Guin's dust-blown world of communal living may strike some as an approximation of Hell, it remains, at the very least, one in which the principle of individual freedom is paramount.

Marge Piercy, *Woman on the Edge of Time*

First published in 1976, *Woman on the Edge of Time* is, perhaps, the most significant feminist utopia yet written, and certainly the most representative of its era. According to some commentators, Piercy's novel marks a 'fundamental break' with utopian tradition, representing the final stage in the evolutionary history of the genre.[6]

Revolving around the central character of Connie Ramos, a thirty-seven year old Mexican-American, unfairly incarcerated in a mental hospital outside New York, *Woman on the Edge of Time* interweaves two stories. On the one hand, it explores the unenviable fate of Connie, one of the victims of present day society, as she fights to maintain her dignity and her mind within an uncaring system. On the other, it uses the device of Connie's medium-like ability to travel through time, to depict society in 2137 and to contrast it with our own. Combining all the major thematic preoccupations of the day, Piercy's utopia is directly engaged with questions of sexual identity, environmental renewal and personal freedom, resulting in an imagined society that appears, at first glance, to resemble a type of counter-cultural commune, where free love, self-expression, and handicrafts are the order of the day. But, in fact, Piercy's pastoral vision is underpinned by highly advanced technology, the apparent benefits of which include completely artificial means of human reproduction that have rendered childbirth obsolete.

Indeed, the central motif of this new society that Connie comes to embrace is the absence of the one factor which, above all others, appears to make her real life so intolerable, namely male oppression. By 2137, gender differences have been all but eliminated: physically, it has become less easy to distinguish between the sexes, and this ambiguity is supported by a language in which the gendered pronouns, 'he' and 'she' have been replaced by 'per' (person). Gender has become irrelevant to the conduct of everyday life, and the traditional family structure has been dismantled. In a world in which the responsibility for childbirth has fallen from the individual to society at large, a biological bond between child and parent is no longer considered necessary or even desirable:

> 'It was part of women's long revolution. When we were breaking all the old hierarchies. Finally there was that one thing we had to give up too, the only power we ever had, in return for no more power for anyone. The original production: the power to give birth. Cause as long as we were biologically enchained, we'd never be equal. And males never would be humanised to be loving and tender. So we all became mothers. Every child has three. To break the nuclear bonding.'
> 'Three! That makes no sense! Three Mothers!'[7]

Inhabiting an eco-friendly community of recycled materials, governed by a system of easy-going anarchy, and adopting a lifestyle of creative endeavour, sexual promiscuity and outdoor pursuits, life in this community named Mattapoisett is a far cry from the urban nightmare that is 1970s New York. Combining a primitive reverence for the natural world with a sophisticated awareness of psychology, genetics and technology, this utopian future has been hard won and the battle is not yet over. The details of how the transition took place are at best sketchy, but by 2137 the remnants of the previous civilisation now inhabit Antarctica, the Moon and platforms in space, from where they continue to launch sporadic attacks upon the Earth. Quite how these peaceable, placid and frequently stoned village-dwellers manage to rouse themselves sufficiently to engage in futuristic warfare with marauding cyborgs is never adequately explained, and these passages are amongst the least satisfactory in the book. Equally puzzling are the fate of the larger part of the Earth's population, which appears to have subsided sufficiently for life to resume on a more manageable scale, and the whereabouts of the manufacturing industry which enables these small communities to equip themselves with such a startling array of futuristic gadgets. But, for all its obvious inconsistencies, *Woman on the Edge of Time* successfully manages to sustain a balance between hope and anger as it switches between genres, utopian optimism and speculative science-fiction repeatedly bracketed within a realist narrative of vivid and systematic torment.

As for Connie, trapped in a situation that recalls the grim satire of Ken Kesey's *One Flew Over the Cookoo's Nest* (1962), her increasingly desperate attempts to escape the confines of the mental ward lead her finally to violent confrontation. Unable to avoid her fate as an experimental guinea-pig for a medical community that cares little for either her sanity or her individuality, the novel ends with an act of revolutionary defiance, as she hits back at her tormenters. What her visions of Mattapoisett ultimately highlight are the horrendous injustices of her own position as a poor, brown-skinned woman in late twentieth-century America — a world that is as incomprehensible to her friends from this benign future, as their world, at least initially, is to her.

Margaret Atwood, *The Handmaid's Tale*

First published in 1985, filmed in 1990 (with a screenplay by Harold Pinter), and even the subject of an opera in 1997, *The Handmaid's Tale* is probably the most widely studied dystopian novel of recent years. Born of a backlash against the feminist ideas which had proved so influential in the preceding decade, Atwood's novel depicts a totalitarian America of the near future, in which women's rights have been totally subjugated to those of a predominantly male ruling class.

Following the assassination of the President and Congress, an act blamed upon Muslim terrorists, the US Constitution is suspended and a state of martial law is imposed. Soon power is in the hands of the Sons of Jacob, a fundamentalist pseudo-Christian organisation which proceeds to strip women of their rights, creating a rigidly controlled theocratic state. It is here, in what is now known as the Republic of Gilead, that the novel's central character Offred (a patronymic, literally 'of-Fred') recounts the tale of her enslavement to this new regime and her attempts to escape.

In this nightmarish future, large tracts of the American continent have been subjected to the effects of nuclear, biological and chemical pollution, rendering much of the population sterile. As a result, society now places a high premium upon fertility and fertile women are an extremely valuable commodity. As one such woman, the options available to Offred are three-fold: if she chooses to rebel against the state, her fate will be execution or deportation to the colonies where, along with lesbians, feminists, nuns, the elderly and 'unwomen' (the infertile), she will succumb to radiation sickness; alternatively, while still young and sexually attractive, she may delay this fate by becoming a 'Jezebel', and work as a prostitute for the ruling elite, a role which the state refuses even to acknowledge; finally, she may choose to undergo re-education prior to becoming a 'Handmaid', a role whose social function is to produce children for the Wives, the partners of the ruling class.

After choosing this latter role, or rather having it chosen for her, Offred is first indoctrinated in the Rachel and Leah Re-Education Center, an institution run by the Aunts, an order of largely sadistic older women acting on behalf of their male superiors. Here, Offred loses not only her name and identity, but is also divorced from all contact with her former family and young child. Now ready to assume her biblical role as handmaid, Offred is placed with the family of the Commander, Fred, and his wife Serena Joy. Here, she has two years to produce a child, before being reassigned to a new family. If, after three such placements, she is unable to produce a healthy child, then the Colonies beckon. In her new role within this family, Offred is to remain largely dormant, her sole function being her regular participation in the 'Ceremony':

The Ceremony goes as usual... Above me, towards the head of the bed, Serena Joy is arranged, outspread. Her legs are apart, I lie between them, my head on her stomach, her pubic bone under the base of my skull, her thighs on either side of me. She too is fully clothed.

My arms are raised; she holds my hands, each of mine in each of hers. This is supposed to signify that we are one flesh, one being. What it really means is that she is in control, of the process and thus of the product. If any. The rings of her left hand cut into my fingers. It may or may not be revenge.

My red skirt is hitched up to my waist, though no higher. Below it the Commander is fucking. What he is fucking is the lower part of my body. I do not say making love, because this is not what he's doing. Copulating too would be inaccurate, because it would imply two people and only one is involved. Nor does rape cover it: nothing is going on here that I haven't signed up for. There wasn't a lot of choice but there was some, and this is what I chose.[8]

In an echo of Huxley's *Brave New World*, the Republic of Gilead is governed by complex sumptuary laws, or dress codes, in which status is reflected through distinctive visual segregation: Commanders wear black; those banished to the Colonies, grey; Wives, blue; their daughters, white; Aunts, brown; the Marthas, or servant class, green; while the Econowives, the partners of low-ranking men, wear a multicoloured dress of red, blue and green, to reflect their multiple role as mother, wife and domestic servant. As for the Handmaids, they are dressed in a red habit and a white headdress that both obscures their vision and prevents them being viewed by others. Rigidly classified and sub-divided according to status, reproductive capacity, and function, the Republic of Gilead creates and encourages resentment and mutual suspicion between categories; a policy of social division fosters an environment of fear and compliance, ensuring the continued dominance of the elite.

Yet, within this closely monitored society, these rules are broken both by the dominant and the subjugated. Soon the Commander, eager to engage in a relationship beyond the confines permitted by the Ceremony, begins to visit Offred in secret; Offred, yearning to feel the intensity of real love, embarks upon an affair with the chauffeur, Nick. As the novel reaches its abrupt conclusion, the black van of the Eyes, or state security, arrives to take Offred away. Has Offred been betrayed or is she being taken to freedom by the underground movement of which Nick claims to be a member? We are denied an answer. In a postscript to the novel, set in 2195, the events of the novel are shown to be the transcript of taped recordings found years after the Republic of Gilead has ceased to exist, as the speakers at an academic conference speculate on Offred's true identity and her fate.

In the end, Atwood's depiction of Gilead is something more than simply an attempt to highlight the dangers of theocratic government. Certainly her principal target is religious fundamentalism and the growing influence of the far-right in contemporary American politics. And yet Atwood also highlights the failings of the feminist move-

ment itself, many of whose more dogmatic pronounce-
ments had come to resemble the rhetoric of those it was
opposing. For the novel also indicates that pre-Gileadian
society was one in which women were denied full control
over their lives, often remaining the subject of physical and
sexual violence. A situation of which Aunt Lydia is quick to
remind Offred: 'There is more than one kind of freedom...
Freedom to and freedom from. In the days of anarchy, it
was freedom to. Now you are being given freedom from.
Don't underrate it.'[9]

JG Ballard, *Kingdom Come*

The most significant voice in dystopian fiction over the last
fifty years, JG Ballard has produced a unique body of work
that catalogues society's deepest fears and anxieties,
mapping the ways in which they continue to fluctuate.
From the 1960s we have his early tales of environmental
catastrophe and psychic regression, *The Drowned World*
(1962), *The Drought* (1964) and *The Crystal World* (1966); the
following decade produced accounts of urban collapse and
deviant sexuality in *The Atrocity Exhibition* (1970), *Crash*
(1973), *Concrete Island* (1974) and *High-Rise* (1975); in more
recent years we have seen an exploration of the unexpected
behavioural consequences of consumerism in *Cocaine Nights*
(1996), *Super-Cannes* (2000) and *Millennium People* (2003).
Throughout this period, however, Ballard's tales of the near
future have maintained an ambiguity of tone in which the
calamitous and the celebratory are wilfully intermingled,
creating a series of texts which persistently question the
boundary between the utopian and its opposite:

I think my work is superficially dystopian, in some respects, but I'm trying to, as you say, affirm a more positive worldview. I lived through more than two-thirds of the last century, which was one of the grimmest epochs in human history – a time of unparalleled human violence and cruelty. Most of my writing was about the 20th century, and anyone writing about the 20th century writes in a dystopian mode without making any effort at all – it just comes with the box of paintbrushes.[10]

Ballard's dystopian outlook is, then, a natural response to the historical epoch against which he is writing, but his attempts to emphasise the unforeseen benefits of outwardly negative experiences, create a clearly identifiable style in which the mundane surface is juxtaposed with the vivid and startling reality that it conceals: 'The suburbs dream of violence. Asleep in their drowsy villas, sheltered by benevolent shopping malls, they wait patiently for the nightmares that will wake them into a more passionate world…'[11]

The opening sentence of the most recent addition to the Ballard canon, *Kingdom Come* (2006), perfectly encapsulates this surreal sense of dislocation, introducing the reader to a world in which the cosy conformities of suburban life are immediately disrupted. *Kingdom Come* is by no means Ballard's finest novel, appearing at times to be little more than a vehicle for ideas better suited to the short story or essay. It is, however, his clearest expression to date of the thesis which has underwritten his work over the last decade, the recognition of an underlying collusion between consumerism and fascism.

Kingdom Come is set in the suburban London town of Brooklands, a fictional zone which informs much of Ballard's work and which mirrors his own fifty-year residence in Shepperton. It is here that Richard Pearson, an unemployed ad-man, comes to investigate the mysterious death of his father a few weeks earlier, shot dead by a deranged mental patient at a shopping mall in the town-centre. Soon enough, Pearson comes to realise that Brooklands' outwardly normal population of sports-obsessed consumerists are in fact on the verge of revolution, as powerful undercurrents of boredom, disaffection and violence are manipulated by a charismatic figure with an apocalyptic agenda. This figure is a washed-up talk-show host named David Cruise, a messianic visionary whose temple is the Metro-Centre, the vast consumerist shrine where Pearson's father was killed. In collusion with other members of the town's middle-class leadership, Cruise is attempting to provoke a violent uprising, a coup in which the untapped forces of consumerism will be harnessed to nationalism to create a new brand of fascism.

With characteristic ambivalence, Ballard's protagonist, Pearson, soon becomes embroiled in the plot, only to find that his loyalties are becoming confused, as his initial antipathy to the shopping-mall and everything it represents becomes blurred and distorted and his own motives become increasingly unclear. Ballard's novel argues that consumerism creates an insatiable demand that can ultimately only be satisfied by fascism. But this is a fascism free from a hard political edge, with slogans and manifestos replaced by more subtle and invasive attempts to create a consumerist hysteria, in which people's hopes and dreams are manipulated to increasingly destructive affect:

> 'This is soft fascism, like the consumer landscape. No goose-stepping, no jackboots, but the same emotions and the same aggression... Who needs liberty and human rights and civic responsibility? What we need is an aesthetics of violence. We believe in the triumph of feelings over reason. Pure materialism isn't enough... We need drama, we need our emotions manipulated, we want to be conned and cajoled. Consumerism fits the bill exactly. It's drawn the blueprint for the fascist states of the future...'[12]

The backdrop to Ballard's tale depicts an England of suburban alienation ringed by anonymous 'motorway towns' in which lives devoid of meaning are given solace by the enormous shopping-malls that dominate the landscape. In tandem with a fervent sporting fanaticism, the consumerist impulse creates a hellish cycle of empty disappointment punctuated by the short-term satisfaction provided by shopping; a nightmarish vision that is manifested through an environment of retail parks and advertising hoardings, monitored by endless CCTV surveillance.

The culmination of the novel sees the Metro-Centre go up in flames, as the mood of frustrated violence finally explodes. Fanatical shoppers take over the mall, taking hostages and fending off the advancing police. But, once again, in a familiar Ballardian manner, the end subverts our expectations and the revolution peters out in entropic fashion. The violence has provoked no transcendent solution and the status quo is resumed. One seeks in vain for a definitive message here, for Ballard's texts always resist any straightforward interpretation. But *Kingdom Come* sounds a cautionary note, if any were needed, to those who believe that an end to the ideological battles of the twentieth-century will enable a utopia of global consumerism in the next.

Notes

[1] Interview with Kurt Vonnegut, *Playboy*, July 1973.

[2] Kurt Vonnegut, *Player Piano* (1952), London: Granada, 1973, p. 255.

[3] Carey, p. 441.

[4] Robin Cook (Derek Raymond), *A State of Denmark*, London: Hutchinson 1970, pp. 125–6.

[5] Ursula K. Le Guin, *The Dispossessed* (1974), London: Grafton, 1975, pp. 296–7.

[6] Perry Anderson, 'The River of Time', *New Left Review* #26, March/April 2004, p. 71 and qtd. in Fredric Jameson, *Archaeologies of the Future: The Desire Called Utopia and Other Science Fictions*, London: Verso, 2005, p. 211.

[7] Marge Piercy, *Woman on the Edge of Time*, London: The Women's Press, 1979, p. 105.

[8] Margaret Atwood, *The Handmaid's Tale* (1985), London: Virago, 1987, p. 104.

[9] Atwood, *Handmaid's Tale*, p. 34.

[10] 'Rattling Other People's Cages: The JG Ballard Interview', Simon Sellars, 29 September 2006 at www.ballardian.com/rattling-other-peoples-cages-the-

jg-ballard-interview

[11] JG Ballard, *Kingdom Come*, London: HarperCollins 2006, p. 3.

[12] Ballard, *Kingdom Come*, p. 168.

Afterword: The Death of Utopia?

Since the end of the Second World War the idea of Utopia has been on the retreat. How, after the gas chambers, could one maintain a belief in human perfectibility or in the promise of an ideal society? The message of the twentieth century appeared to be that, regardless of man's ingenuity and the undeniable benefits of technological progress, human nature remained both essentially flawed and stubbornly resistant to change. The utopian tradition had exhausted itself, as expressions of the future became uniformly dark reflections of our deepest fears and anxieties.

In a reflection of this shift, the post-war years saw a raft of publications proclaiming the end not only of utopia, but also to the ideological conflicts through which it had been sustained: Judith N Shklar's *After Utopia: The Decline of Political Faith* (1957) was soon followed by Daniel Bell's *The End of Ideology: On the Exhaustion of Political Ideas in the Fifties* (1962). But it was a lecture given by Herbert Marcuse in 1967, and published the same year as *Das Ende der Utopie*, or *The End of Utopia*, that seemed to put the nail in the coffin. Indeed, not only did Marcuse suggest that the concept of utopia was now inapplicable to human affairs, he also argued that we had now reached the 'end of history', at least in as far as history could be interpreted as continuous human progress.[1]

Of course, in the following decade, the beleaguered concept of utopia was to stage something of a comeback, as new political movements promoting racial and sexual identity, as well as those supporting environmental change, turned to utopianism as a vehicle for political and aesthetic expression. This revival was short-lived, however, and by the end of the 1980s, Marcuse's claims were to be echoed by Francis Fukuyama in his celebrated essay *The End of History?* (1989). The claim by Fukuyama that history was at an end was, in fact, not so much a denial of utopianism, as an acknowledgement that utopia had finally arrived. For Fukuyama believed, in essence, that the great ideological conflict between left and right, between Communism and Capitalism, was now at an end. Capitalism had won. The ideological impetus driving history had been brought to its conclusion and the free market was now free to assert its rightful global hegemony.

Needless to say, the idea that we had reached our final destination and that it was nineties-style American liberalism, was unacceptable to many, amongst them the British philosopher John Gray. Gray, a sometime Thatcherite, occasional Blairite, and a consistent opponent of utopian thinking in all its forms, believes that any attempt to harness history towards some final end, regardless of its ideological basis, is doomed to failure. Indeed, he goes further, arguing that not only is utopia impossible to achieve, but the very attempt to realise it is itself the root of untold misery and suffering. According to Gray, today's Utopian thinkers are hopelessly deluded secular millennialists, who, displaying the same religious fervour as their medieval counterparts, cling to a dogmatic belief in the possibility of an historical End of Days, when God's intentions, or, in his absence, their own beliefs, will finally be realised. Now an end has come, but it is an end to such misplaced beliefs:

> The faith in Utopia, which killed so many in the centuries following the French Revolution, is dead. Like other faiths it may be resurrected in circumstances that cannot be foreseen; but it is unlikely to trouble us much further in the next few decades. The cycle in which world politics was dominated by secular versions of apocalyptic myth has come to an end, and, in an historic reversal, old-time religion has re-emerged at the heart of global conflict.[2]

According to Gray, in his recent book, *Black Mass: Apocalyptic Religion and the Death of Utopia* (2007), the taint of utopianism and its impossible dreams has underwritten the entire Enlightenment project. The Golden Age of utopia, or at least the period of the greatest utopian expression, falls broadly between 1790 and 1920, and coincides historically with an era of dominant Enlightenment values. That such an era should have been succeeded by a predominantly dystopian age, suggests, to Gray at least, that beyond our simple mistrust of technological progress, Enlightenment values have been exposed as bearing the responsibility for the ideological excesses we have witnessed over the course of the last century. During this period, dystopias from Huxley to Orwell, Wells to Ballard, have, quite rightly, signalled to us the 'ugly reality that results from pursuing unrealizable dreams'.[3]

Gray's assault upon utopianism is supported, from a different direction, by Russell Jacoby, whose *The End of Utopia: Politics and Culture in an Age of Apathy* (2000) argues, not as Gray does, that Utopianism is a pernicious doctrine, but instead claims that it is simply an exhausted one. Jacoby argues that a widespread failure of the imagination has taken hold in Western societies. Unable to grasp the vision of a radical future that animated previous generations, today's would-be utopians have lost their revolutionary zeal, and are now content to retreat into the intellectual backwater of largely incoherent academic theories with little or no practical application. But is utopianism really as pernicious a doctrine as Gray suggests? And has it really run out of steam?

As the twenty-first century unfolds, the concept of utopia remains hopelessly mired in the ideological battles of the twentieth, unable to extricate itself from an unwanted association with the horrors of Auschwitz and the Gulag. Yet, equally, an understandable reluctance to re-engage with the grand political projects of the past is interpreted, today, as an unacceptable loss of political vision. In his essay, 'The Politics of Utopia' (2004), the cultural theorist Fredric Jameson asks, 'Does this peculiar entity still have a social function?' He suggests that the unparalleled and unimaginable technological advances of the last century may well have rendered the term utopia obsolete, as reality effectively outstrips our ability to depict the future.[4] Utopia has fallen victim, Jameson claims, to the weakening sense of history which accompanies postmodernity, to the point where, paradoxically, it now finds itself regarded as either too political (sinister, totalitarian), or not political enough (idealist, impractical).[5] 'Utopias are non-fictional', he concludes, 'even though they are non-existent. Utopias in fact come to us as barely audible messages from a future that may never come into being.'[6] And perhaps it is this perspective which best allows us to sidestep the quagmire into which utopia has sunk. For, if the multiplicity of utopian worlds which we have touched upon here may be viewed as existing somewhere between the realms of fiction and reality, occupying endless possible futures which may, or may not, yet come into being, then the utopian project, far from being exhausted, is, on the contrary, boundless, illimitable.

The clamour of discordant voices that continues to surround the idea of utopia has had the welcome effect of ensuring that the utopian tradition maintains its position at the forefront of the public imagination. And amidst the claims that utopia is, or at least ought to be, on its deathbed, one suspects that this debate is one that has been replayed throughout its history, and one which, despite claims to the contrary, is likely to persist. For as Krishan Kumar has suggested, the utopian impulse is deeply grounded within the human imagination and without it much of our impetus towards a better future would be lost:

> I don't wish to defend everything that has been done in the name of utopia. But I think that many of the attacks misconceive its nature and function... utopia is not mainly about providing detailed blueprints for social reconstruction. Its concern with ends is about making us think about possible worlds. It is about inventing and imagining worlds for our contempla-

tion and delight. It opens up our minds to the possibilities of the human condition. It is this that we most seem to need at the present time. There are doomsters enough – though they have their part to play, like the prophets of old, warning and admonishing. There are also our latter-day millenarians, somewhat jaded in their outlook on the world, and rather prepared to settle for a quiet life and the idle ticking-over of the engine of history. Without wishing to bang the inspiration drum too loudly, this hardly seems enough.[7]

Notes

1 Herbert Marcuse, *The End of Utopia* (1967) at http://www.marxists.org/reference/archive/marcuse/works/1967/end-utopia.htm

2 John Gray, *Black Mass: Apocalyptic Religion and the Death of Utopia*, London: Penguin 2007, p. 184.

3 Gray, p. 20.

4 Fredric Jameson, 'The Politics of Utopia', *New Left Review*, #25 Jan/Feb 2004, 35–54, p. 35.

5 Jameson, p. 42.

6 Jameson, p. 54.

7 Krishan Kumar, 'Apocalypse, Millennium and Utopia Today', in Malcolm Bull, ed., *Apocalypse Theory and the Ends of the World*, Oxford: Blackwell, 1995, 200–224, p. 219.

Further Reading

Alexander, Peter, and Gill, Roger, eds., *Utopias*, London: Duckworth, 1984

Baccolini, Raffaella & Moylan, Tom, eds., *Dark Horizons: Science Fiction and the Dystopian Imagination*, London: Routledge, 2003

Bartkowski, Frances, *Feminist Utopias*, Lincoln, NE: University of Nebraska Press, 1989

Bell, Daniel, *The End of Ideology: On the Exhaustion of Political Ideas in the Fifties* (1962), Cambridge, MA: Harvard University Press, 2000

Black, Jonathan, *The Secret History of the World*, London: Quercus, 2008

Bruce, Susan, ed., *Three Early Modern Utopias: Utopia, New Atlantis, The Isle of Pines*, Oxford: OUP, 1999

Bull, Malcolm ed., *Apocalypse Theory and the Ends of the World*, Oxford: Blackwell, 1995

Carey, John, ed., *The Faber Book of Utopias*, London: Faber, 1999

Claeys, Gregory & Sargent, Lyman Tower, eds., *The Utopia Reader*, New York: New York University Press, 1999

Coates, Chris, *Utopia Britannica: British Utopian Experiments: 1325–1945*, London: Diggers and Dreamers Publications, 2001

Cohn, Norman, *The Pursuit of the Millennium: A History of Popular Religious and Social Movements in Europe from the*

Eleventh to the Sixteenth Century, London: Secker & Warburg, 1957

Conrad, Peter, *Islands: A Trip Through Space and Time*, London: Thames & Hudson, 2009

Curran, Bob, *Lost Lands, Forgotten Realms: Sunken Continents, Vanished Cities, and the Kingdoms that History Misplaced*, Franklin Lakes, NJ: New Page Books, 2007

Darley, Gillian, *Villages of Vision: A Study of Strange Utopias* (1975), Nottingham: Five Leaves Publications, 2007

Davis, JC, *Utopia and the Ideal Society: A Study of English Utopian Writing 1516–1700*, Cambridge: Cambridge University Press, 1981

Elliot, Robert C., *The Shape of Utopia: Studies in a Literary Genre*, Chicago: Chicago University Press, 1970

Ferguson, John, *Utopias of the Classical World*, London: Thames & Hudson, 1975

Fukuyama, Francis, *The End of History and the Last Man*, London: Penguin, 1992

Goodwin, Barbara & Taylor, Keith, *The Politics of Utopia: A Study in Theory and Practice*, London: Hutchinson, 1982

Gray, John, *Black Mass: Apocalyptic Religion and the Death of Utopia*, London: Allen Lane, 2007

Jacoby, Russell, *The End of Utopia: Politics and Culture in an Age of Apathy*, New York: Basic Books, 2000

Jameson, Fredric, *Archaeologies of the Future: The Desire Called Utopia and Other Science Fictions*, London: Verso, 2005

Kumar, Krishan, *Utopia and Anti-Utopia in Modern Times*, Oxford: Blackwell, 1987

Levin, Bernard, *A World Elsewhere*, London: Jonathan Cape, 1994

Manguel, Alberto & Guadalupi, Gianni, eds., *The Dictionary of Imaginary Places*, London: Bloomsbury, 1999

Manuel, Frank E. & Manuel, Fritzie P., *Utopian Thought in the Western World*, Oxford: Blackwell, 1979

Marcuse, Herbert, 'The End of Utopia', in *Five Lectures: Psychoanalysis, Politics and Utopia* (1967), Boston MA: Beacon Press, 1970

More, Thomas, *Utopia* (1516), ed. by Paul Turner, London: Penguin, 1965

Moylan, Tom, *Demand the Impossible: Science Fiction and the Utopian Imagination*, London: Methuen, 1986

Mumford, Lewis, *The Story of Utopias: Ideal Commonwealths and Social Myths*, London: Harrap, 1923

Neville-Sington, Pamela & Sington, David, *Paradise Dreamed: How Utopian Thinkers Have Changed the Modern World*, London: Bloomsbury, 1993

Rees, Christine, *Eighteenth-Century Utopian Fiction*, London: Longman, 1995

Rennie, Neil, *Far-Fetched Facts: The Literature of Travel and the Idea of the South Seas*, London: Clarendon Press, 1998

Sargent, Lyman Tower, *British and American Utopian Literature, 1516–1985: An Annotated, Chronological Bibliography*, Boston: GK Hall, 1979

Shklar, Judith N, *After Utopia: The Decline of Political Faith*, Princeton, NJ: University of Princeton Press, 1957

Snodgrass, Mary Ellen, *The Encyclopedia of Utopian Literature*, Santa Barbara, CA: Abc-Clio, 1995

Standish, David, *Hollow Earth: The Long and Curious History of Imagining Strange Lands, Fantastical Creatures, Advanced*

Civilizations and Marvelous Machines Below the Earth's Surface, Cambridge MA: Da Capo Press, 2006

Trahair, Richard CS, *Utopias and Utopians: An Historical Dictionary*, London: Fitzroy Dearborn, 1999

Websites

Utopian Studies Society
www.utopianstudieseurope.org/index.php
Utopia on the Internet – Philosophy for a Better World
www.erols.com/jonwill/utopialist.htm
Utopian Writing 1516–1798
www.trin.cam.ac.uk/rws1001/utopia/default.htm
The Society for Utopian Studies
www.utoronto.ca/utopia/
Utopia Britannica
www.utopia-britannica.org.uk/pages/homebase.htm
New York Public Library: Utopia – The Search for the Ideal
   Society in the Western World
http://utopia.nypl.org/homepage_qt.html
The British Library: Citizenship – Dreamers & Dissenters
www.bl.uk/learning/histcitizen/21cc/utopia/utopia.html
Utopia Links
www.geocities.com/solarcereal/index.html
Utopia Online Library
www.deepleafproductions.com/utopialibrary/

Index